IT NEVER HAPPEN

Torben Betts

IT NEVER HAPPENED

or

STATE TERROR IN EIGHT EASY STAGES

OBERON BOOKS
LONDON

WWW.OBERONBOOKS.COM

First published in 2019 by Oberon Books Ltd
521 Caledonian Road, London N7 9RH
Tel: +44 (0) 20 7607 3637 / Fax: +44 (0) 20 7607 3629
e-mail: info@oberonbooks.com
www.oberonbooks.com

PB ISBN: 9781786827777
E ISBN: 9781786827760

Cover design: Spy Studio

eBook conversion by Lapiz Digital Services, India.

10 9 8 7 6 5 4 3 2 1

For Victoria
with thanks for twenty-four years of love, faith and support

"It never happened. Nothing ever happened.
Even while it was happening, it wasn't happening.
It didn't matter. It was of no interest."
HAROLD PINTER

THE EIGHT EASY STAGES

DRAMATIS PERSONAE

I. The Free Liberal Media

WICKHAM, a salaried journalist

SNIDE, another one

YOUNG, an idealist

II. A Civil Servant's Shoes

SWINTON, a killer

PRUDHOE, a killer

DUNS, a victim of the system

PAXTON, a pillar of the Establishment

III. The Mother of All Conspiracy Theories

DIETER, a Nazi

FRIEDA, a Nazi

HEINRICH, a Nazi

LOTTE, a Nazi

MAX, a Doctor of Philosophy

IV. Old Men Talking, Young Men Dying
FRANK, a human sacrifice
ARTHUR, another one
JULIET, a lady of the night
BEATRICE, a singer

V. Pointing Towards the Future
ANNA-MARIE, a sculptress
LUDWIG, a war hero
OTTO, a crown prince
LARA, his betrothed

VI. Punching Down in Patriarchal Systems
SIR PHILIP, a nobleman
LADY MARY, a noblewoman
LUCY, their servant

VII. The Things We Do For Love
HACKER, a foul-mouthed butcher
MRS FITZWILLIAM, a wealthy Catholic
JOHNS, her assistant

VIII. Bloody Women
KATHERINE, a distressed queen
THOMAS, her would-be lover
SIR ROBERT, a completely charmless man

It Never Happened was first performed on 14th May 2019
at ArtsEd, London. The cast was as follows:

I. The Free Liberal Media
WICKHAM, Lizzie Back
SNIDE, Anna Warke
YOUNG, Colette O'Brien

II. A Civil Servant's Shoes
SWINTON, Charlie Derrar
PRUDHOE, Danny Sykes
DUNS, Josh Miller
PAXTON, Phoebe Delikoura

III. The Mother of All Conspiracy Theories
DIETER, Michael Workeye
FRIEDA, Leah Shine
HEINRICH, Josh Miller
LOTTE, Colette O'Brien
MAX, Danny Sykes

IV. Old Men Talking, Young Men Dying
FRANK, James Westphal
ARTHUR, Ben Castle-Gibb
JULIET, Hannah Richardson
BEATRICE, Shelby Carling

V. Pointing Towards the Future
ANNA-MARIE, Lizzie Back
LUDWIG, Ben Castle-Gibb
OTTO, Josh Miller
LARA, Anna Warke

VI. Punching Down in Patriarchal Systems
SIR PHILIP, Charlie Derrar
LADY MARY, Shelby Carling
LUCY, Rachel Nwokoro

VII. The Things We Do For Love
HACKER, Michael Workeye
MRS FITZWILLIAM, Hannah Richardson
JOHNS, Leah Shine

VIII. Bloody Women
KATHERINE, Phoebe Delikoura
THOMAS, James Westphal
SIR ROBERT, Ben Castle-Gibb

Director, Alex Thorpe
Designer, Anna Reid
Lighting, Sam Waddington
Sound, Eamonn O'Dwyer
Production Manager, Di Stedman
Stage Manager, Alex James
DSM, Sarah Lyndon
Costume Supervisor, Åse Amy Djärf
Costume Assistant, Marianne Harwich
Construction Manager, Sean Flynn
Master Carpenter, Dan Cheyne
Chief Technician, Phil Bell
Technician, Christopher Mould

Director of the School of Acting, Julie Spencer
Voice and Dialect, Mike Hayden
Movement, Gail Sixsmith

With special thanks to Gareth Farr and Matthew Dunster

I. THE FREE LIBERAL MEDIA

WICKHAM at a desk, clearly playing some form of game. YOUNG stands to one side, waiting for him/her to finish.

WICKHAM: So here I am, this intrepid little monkey, swinging through the trees, swinging from vine to vine, all these vicious crocodiles snapping away beneath me, ready to devour me should I fall, with no safety net whatsoever. And so what I have to do is land on these ledges here and then collect all the gold coins before this big, bad wolf appears and knocks me down into the swamp below.

YOUNG: I was told you wanted to see me?

WICKHAM: Honestly, the people who come up with these games, it's utter genius, if you ask me. And to *create* the idea is one thing but to then actually *design* it. To then make it real-world. It's simply incredible.

YOUNG: Of course.

WICKHAM: And it's not just being a *technical* genius, is it, because you really have to *know* and to *understand* the human brain, you really have to get *under the skin* of human beings, you have to be something of a psychologist to know how our minds work, to know exactly how to create the kind of addictive, timewasting game we're all going to want to play again and again and again and again.

YOUNG: I'm not really a fan of such things.

WICKHAM: When what we *should* be doing is working.

YOUNG: Yes.

WICKHAM: These guys must be rolling in it like pigs in the proverbial. I was just saying to the other newbie, I was just saying that journalism these days is a mugs' game. If it's untold riches you crave. Because it's information

technology, social media, computer software design, that
kind of thing, that's where the big bucks lie, not this racket.

YOUNG: I'm not especially interested in…

WICKHAM: If chasing the Yankee dollar is what ye seek,
I said best change professions forthwith.

YOUNG: I'll bear that in mind.

WICKHAM: Or banking or the law, I told him.

YOUNG: Right.

WICKHAM: But that goes without saying.

YOUNG: Of course it does.

WICKHAM: I've got chums who graduated with far worse
degrees than I, at far inferior places of education, already
on six-figure salaries, working in the City.

YOUNG: Money has never really been my motivation so…

WICKHAM: We are talking a hundred grand per annum, when
you're only in your mid-twenties and, with all due respect
to both of them, they're neither of them the sharpest tools
in the tray, and already they've got lifestyles I can only
dream about.

YOUNG: Do you think this'll take long?

WICKHAM: A lovely flat in the Docklands, a thirty-grand
Beemer in the garage, eating out in classy restaurants
every single night of their lives!

YOUNG: Only I've got a deadline to…

WICKHAM: *(To the PC.)* Oh, *quel dommage*, I am once again
lunch for the gluttonous crocodiles!

YOUNG: And then I've got an interview after that so…

WICKHAM: *(Faux posh.)* But still…ours is a noble calling, what?

YOUNG: Hopefully, yes.

WICKHAM: Speaking truth to power et cetera.

YOUNG: Serving the people, yes.

Enter SNIDE.

SNIDE: So sorry I'm late.

WICKHAM: Alright, boss?

SNIDE: Meeting after meeting after meeting after meeting.

WICKHAM: The bane of our lives.

SNIDE: When what I'd actually like to do one day is some journalism for a change.

WICKHAM: Oh, absolutely.

SNIDE: If you ever want to piss ninety minutes of your life away then try sitting yourself down in a roomful of advertising people and airline executives.

WICKHAM: I shall bear that mind.

SNIDE: The said airline executives are not best pleased about the feature we ran last week about climate change.

WICKHAM: We've had our knuckles rapped there a few times.

SNIDE: But I'm thinking, hello, we're only trying to save the planet here.

WICKHAM: Guilty as charged!

YOUNG: I was just wondering if…

SNIDE: Upshot is we have to scale back any future articles connecting global warming to the burning of fossil fuels or face losing half our advertising revenue.

WICKHAM: Ouch!

SNIDE: Ouch indeed, my friend.

YOUNG: Just wondering if there was any chance we could have this meeting *after* lunch because…

SNIDE: Where d'you fancy eating today incidentally?

WICKHAM: Your turn to choose.

SNIDE: There's an Italian just opened which is very good apparently?

WICKHAM: Then Italian it shall be.

SNIDE: *You* like Italian food?

YOUNG: Of course but…

SNIDE: Nothing better than a good pepperoni pizza, is there?

YOUNG: I'm a vegan actually so…

SNIDE: Of course you are…

WICKHAM: Goes without saying.

YOUNG: Anyway, you wanted to see me?

SNIDE: Indeed we do.

WICKHAM: So draw up a pew.

YOUNG: I'd rather stand.

SNIDE: Fact is…

WICKHAM: And to cut a long story…

SNIDE: …a very long story…

WICKHAM: …short.

SNIDE: Your latest piece is…

SNIDE/WICKHAM: …not really what we're after.

A silence.

YOUNG: You're joking?

SNIDE: Do we look like we're joking?

WICKHAM: *You* certainly *don't* look like you're joking…

SNIDE: And neither do you.

SNIDE/WICKHAM: So there's your answer.

YOUNG: What I mean is…

SNIDE: You state in your opening paragraph that the army is 'repeatedly massacring unarmed civilians who are protesting the illegal military occupation'.

YOUNG: That's because it is.

WICKHAM: That's merely one way of *looking* at it.

SNIDE: You also say that in one month they've killed with impunity journalists, paramedics, the elderly and, it is estimated, at least twenty-two children under the age of sixteen.

YOUNG: That's because they have.

SNIDE: You also describe these events…

WICKHAM: …which are admittedly tragic.

SNIDE: …as 'crimes'.

YOUNG: That's because they are.

SNIDE/WICKHAM: We need to re-examine our terminology.

YOUNG: I'm simply stating the facts.

SNIDE: The facts according to *you.*

YOUNG: It *is* an illegal occupation, as recognised under international law, it *was* a massacre and these *were* unarmed civilians so…

SNIDE: *Some* of them were unarmed.

YOUNG: *All* of them were.

SNIDE: Not according to my sources.

YOUNG: Who are your sources?

SNIDE/WICKHAM: That we're not at liberty to divulge.

YOUNG: Well, I've seen the film evidence and amongst all the blood and the blackened corpses, they found not one grenade, not one gun, not even a child's catapult!

SNIDE: Okay, but you cannot call this a crime.

YOUNG: Well, I'm going to.

SNIDE: Then we won't run with it.

YOUNG: What do we call it then?

SNIDE: I dunno. A clash?

YOUNG: A clash?

WICKHAM: Or what about a border skirmish?

SNIDE: Now that I prefer.

WICKHAM: Then border skirmish it shall be.

SNIDE: Both sides as bad as each other kind of thing?

WICKHAM: Both need their heads banging together?

SNIDE: Always two sides to every story.

WICKHAM: Basic rule of journalism.

YOUNG: But replicating government press notices is surely *not* journalism?

SNIDE: It's *their* version of events so…

YOUNG: Relaying what those in power are presenting as the truth is surely *not*…?

SNIDE: You are letting your emotions get in the way of your…

WICKHAM: …subjectivity.

SNIDE: Your sense of balance.

WICKHAM: Exactly.

YOUNG: While there *are* two groups of people involved out there: only *one* is doing the killing and only *one* is doing the dying.

SNIDE: If you don't mind me saying so, you're being a tiny bit…

WICKHAM: Naïve.

SNIDE: Jejune.

WICKHAM: Nice adjective.

SNIDE: Thank you.

YOUNG: In what way…?

SNIDE: Jejune?

WICKHAM: Je-june.

SNIDE: Jejune because we live in a rough and tumble world.

WICKHAM: Jejune because the said world is complex.

SNIDE: Jejune because morality is always…

WICKHAM: Hard to define?

SNIDE: Exactly.

YOUNG: All I'm doing is telling the truth.

SNIDE: But as you must surely know…

WICKHAM: One man's truth…

SNIDE: …is another man's falsehood.

WICKHAM: And vice versa.

SNIDE: Et cetera, et cetera…

YOUNG: But whenever Westminster's official enemies are killing civilians, or *allegedly* killing civilians, then we run front page editorials for weeks demanding military intervention?

SNIDE: Yes, but it's not quite…

WICKHAM: …as simple as that.

YOUNG: But our *allies* can carry on murdering who they like so long as they keep buying our weapons, selling us oil on the cheap and doing our bidding.

A silence.

WICKHAM: Are you sure a career in journalism is quite right for you?

SNIDE: We, as you know, are a left-leaning, liberal-minded establishment…

WICKHAM: But there *are* certain pressures we are working under…

SNIDE: Commercial pressures for one.

WICKHAM: As we've already stated.

SNIDE: Sadly with our circulation falling…

WICKHAM: We rely more and more on advertising revenues for our…

SNIDE: Survival.

WICKHAM: Which is what it all boils down to.

SNIDE: At the end of the day.

WICKHAM: *Au fin du jour.*

SNIDE: Which is, for your information…

SNIDE/WICKHAM: …French.

YOUNG: But we're supposed to be independent of all that surely?

SNIDE and WICKHAM laugh until they can laugh no more.

Why is that funny?

SNIDE: I can honestly say…

WICKHAM: Hand on heart.

SNIDE: And as two journalists with just a little more experience than you…

SNIDE/WICKHAM: That we do think here with our own minds…

SNIDE: And we have never once…

WICKHAM: Been told what to write.

SNIDE: By anyone.

YOUNG: That's because they don't *have* to tell you.

SNIDE/WICKHAM: Don't they?

YOUNG: You've already internalised the values of the system.

SNIDE/WICKHAM: What system?

WICKHAM: And anyway these 'people' you seek to serve so much are far more interested in what kind of dress the princess will be wearing tomorrow.

SNIDE: You *are* aware there's a royal wedding taking place *au matin*?

WICKHAM: And she is going to look radiant.

SNIDE: The great hope of the nation.

YOUNG: Are you being serious?

SNIDE: And we have the wishes of our readers...

WICKHAM: Our subscribers.

SNIDE: ...to think of.

WICKHAM: So a big front page photo of a beautiful, young brunette...

SNIDE: ...is going to shift a few more copies than one of...

WICKHAM: ...a few hundred corpses in the sand.

YOUNG: This paper used to be a beacon of light in the darkness of this world.

SNIDE: And it still is.

WICKHAM: Otherwise we wouldn't want to work here.

YOUNG: But now it's just a PR arm of the government.

SNIDE: We challenge the government on every issue.

YOUNG: The editor was best man at the Prime Minister's wedding!

SNIDE: One is free to be friends with whomever one wishes.

YOUNG: His latest book is dedicated to him!

SNIDE: And have you read the aforementioned book?

WICKHAM: His brilliant…

SNIDE: Quite brilliant.

YOUNG: But utterly fawning.

WICKHAM: …biography of Churchill?

SNIDE/WICKHAM: The greatest Englishman to ever live.

YOUNG: A genocidal, racist, drunken, white supremacist snob.

SNIDE/WICKHAM: But one to whom we owe the freedoms we all enjoy today!

A silence.

SNIDE: All this really does go to show that…

WICKHAM: It underlines the fact most clearly that…

SNIDE: …you are somewhat…

WICKHAM: …out of place here.

SNIDE: And that you maybe should…

WICKHAM: …be plying your trade…

SNIDE: …elsewhere…

WICKHAM: Somewhere a little less…

SNIDE/WICKHAM: Salaried.

YOUNG: Salaried?

SNIDE/WICKHAM: Salaried.

SNIDE: Because once you do accept a salary there are certain…

WICKHAM: Conditions…

SNIDE: And standards…

WICKHAM: That need to be met.

SNIDE: And so, without any further ado…

WICKHAM: It is our sad duty to relate that…

SNIDE: …the management's decision is…

WICKHAM: …to offer you a very generous…

SNIDE/WICKHAM: …redundancy package.

A long silence.

YOUNG: You're firing me?

SNIDE: This was only ever a trial period.

WICKHAM: But because we recognise your talents…

SNIDE: We don't want to cast you adrift…

WICKHAM: …into the insecure world…

SNIDE: …of the freelancer…

WICKHAM: Without a penny to your name so….

SNIDE: It's not a massive amount but…

A long silence as a cheque is proffered.

YOUNG: *(Taking it.)* Please, I really need this job.

SNIDE: That we do appreciate.

YOUNG: We've just bought a property.

SNIDE/WICKHAM: And we *both* know the stresses of that.

YOUNG: We're getting married in a month…

SNIDE/WICKHAM: We all have choices.

YOUNG: Is this decision final?

SNIDE: Well, what can we say, if you *could* learn to bend to the real world a little?

WICKHAM: Not rock our happy little boat quite so much then…

SNIDE: Who knows?

YOUNG: We've just taken out a mortgage.

SNIDE: It's merely a question of horses for courses.

WICKHAM: A career is currently in the balance.

SNIDE: A careful decision being made.

WICKHAM: To be part of the company.

SNIDE: A valued member of the team.

WICKHAM: A pension, and holidays.

SNIDE: Money each month.

WICKHAM: Or to go it alone.

SNIDE: To live off one's wits.

WICKHAM: To follow one's bliss.

SNIDE: This new life of yours *has* been very hard fought for, hasn't it?

WICKHAM: Very hard won.

SNIDE: So can you really now return to…

WICKHAM: …financial insecurity?

SNIDE: Can you walk the tightrope of your own talent out there alone, with no safety net beneath you?

A silence as YOUNG battles her rage. Then:

YOUNG: *(A sudden passion.)* You have no idea what my life's been like! You, who sail through your existence on the blind conveyor belt of your own privilege! They destroyed the industry in my hometown, killed the self-respect of its people, slowly murdered our community. It was a deliberate social cleansing of the poor, which continues to this day. I was the first in my family ever to get to college and what motivated me was anger, was to be a voice for the voiceless, to stand up for the oppressed. And now that I'm finally here, in a place that should be a force for all things noble and all things decent, this, this, this is what I find!? It's not good enough, is it? It's nowhere near good enough! Because all we have in this life is the truth, all we have in this life is the truth and our compassion for others and we're destroying the planet and we're destroying all its precious lifeforms and so one day and soon we're going to destroy ourselves and we should be screaming all this loudly from the rooftops every single day of our lives and so yes, I shall! I *shall* walk the tightrope of my own talent out there, out there in the cold brutality of the real world. I shall never ever sell my soul!

She turns and storms away.

SNIDE: We could move you from foreign affairs?

WICKHAM: To be our top royal correspondent!

SNIDE: It would double your wages?

WICKHAM: From a small fish there to a big fish here.

YOUNG stops in her tracks. Turns.

SNIDE: You could cover the wedding tomorrow.

WICKHAM: Go into detail about that dress.

SNIDE: Interview the designer.

WICKHAM: Take photos of the morons waving flags.

YOUNG approaches the others.

SNIDE: Remember: we are selling a product.

WICKHAM: We need to improve our circulation.

SNIDE: To attract more advertising cash.

WICKHAM: To please our shareholders.

SNIDE: To make the great world spin.

WICKHAM: No evil to expose.

SNIDE: Just reporting on conditions.

YOUNG: It is of course an honour and a privilege to be employed by this fine and upstanding newspaper.

YOUNG returns the cheque and then leaves.

SNIDE: Now that is one very smart kid.

WICKHAM: Will go far in this world.

SNIDE: Without a shadow of doubt.

WICKHAM: Time for lunch?

SNIDE: Time for lunch.

SNIDE/WICKHAM: It is always, always time for lunch.

II. A CIVIL SERVANT'S SHOES

The Beatles ('Please, Please Me') on a transistor radio. DUNS, gagged, is tied to a chair. SWINTON and PRUDHOE are gambling over cards, using a crate. SWINTON is cleaning up.

SWINTON: What is this utter drivel?

PRUDHOE: These cards, man!

SWINTON: The way music's going these days.

PRUDHOE: It's like I'm cursed or someing.

SWINTON: The final collapse of civilisation as we know it.

PRUDHOE: Deal then.

SWINTON: And I use the word music in the broadest possible sense.

PRUDHOE: Come on!

SWINTON: How can you compare this to a Schubert string quartet or a bit of long, complicated jazz?

PRUDHOE: It's The Beatles, innit?

SWINTON: The who?

PRUDHOE: You're so outta touch!

SWINTON: And how do they let this on the radio anyway… it's complete filth!

PRUDHOE: No, it ain't!

SWINTON: Just listen to the words they're singin'!?

PRUDHOE: I don't care what they're singin'!

SWINTON: 'Please please me like I please you.'

PRUDHOE: So?

SWINTON: He's trying to get her to go down on him, in'e?

PRUDHOE: Is he?

SWINTON: He's saying I'm sick of goin down on you all the time and getting jaw ache when you don't do nuffin whatsoever for me in that department.

PRUDHOE: You're reading too much into it…

SWINTON: Just listen to the words.

They listen to the words.

PRUDHOE: Now I come to think of it…

SWINTON: 'You don't need me to show the way, love.'

PRUDHOE: But how can he go down on himself?

SWINTON: *Homo Sapiens* lacks the spinal flexibility for such an act.

PRUDHOE: Can't ever get Pauline to go down on *me*.

SWINTON: Which is no doubt why you're such an enthusiastic employer of prostitutes.

PRUDHOE: She says it's nasty.

SWINTON: And that's what these Beatles are on about. It's like 'e knows she's only *pretendin'* to be all prim and proper 'cos she don't want him to fink she's a slut but really she knows perfectly well how to provide oral relief and so what 'e's sayin is come on darlin let's cut out the angel act and maybe try a 69.

PRUDHOE: What's that?

SWINTON: That's when 'e goes down on 'er at the same time as she goes down on im.

PRUDHOE: Chance'd be a fine thing.

SWINTON: This rock n'roll is always sex, sex, sex.

PRUDHOE: So?

SWINTON: There are some things in life far more important.

PRUDHOE: Twist.

SWINTON: Money, for example.

PRUDHOE: Deal again.

SWINTON: I'm cleaning you out ere.

SWINTON starts dealing.

You sure you don't want to cut your losses?

PRUDHOE: Twist.

SWINTON: You're just frowin good money after bad now.

PRUDHOE: I'm savin' up!

SWINTON: You gotta learn how to exercise restraint.

PRUDHOE: I'm savin' up so's I can quit this life.

SWINTON: Otherwise you'll never get nowhere.

PRUDHOE: Got me eye on an old farm.

SWINTON: You been sayin' this for ages now.

PRUDHOE: Still need a few grand.

SWINTON: We undertook this insecure mode of employment in the full knowledge…

PRUDHOE: Me and Pauline are gonna live off the land.

SWINTON: …that we were goin without paid holiday, sick leave and any form of pension…

PRUDHOE: Grow our own vegetables.

SWINTON: …that might mean we'd be able to retire from this line of work some day and put up our feet, so to speak.

PRUDHOE: These cards are rigged!

SWINTON: Shuffle at your leisure.

PRUDHOE: I will, mate!

PRUDHOE shuffles the pack.

SWINTON: So, knowin' all this, the man who exercises restraint, who actually *respects* money, and women for that matter, that is to say someone like meself…

PRUDHOE: It's 'cos I'm tired of all this killin.

SWINTON: 'e puts money in the pot for a rainy day, 'e is prudent, 'e is careful, 'e don't live only for is pay day on a Friday and piss every penny away on gamblin', prostitutes and Johnny Walker Red Label.

PRUDHOE: I wanna find some meanin'. Twist.

SWINTON: Which is what makes us two so different.

PRUDHOE: Fuck it!

SWINTON: Do *I* have an alcohol addiction?

PRUDHOE: *(Wanting another deal.)* Gotta get out of the city.

SWINTON: No, I do not.

PRUDHOE: Feel the rays of the sun on me face.

SWINTON: Do *I* spend all of my downtime in gamblin' dens, brothels?

PRUDHOE: *(Wanting another twist.)* I need some redemption.

SWINTON: No, I do not.

PRUDHOE: *(Wanting another twist.)* What I really need is some redemption!

SWINTON: Am *I* forever smearing ointment on my slippery testicles…

PRUDHOE: *(Wanting another twist.)* Gonna seek solace in nature.

SWINTON: *(Twisting.)* …so's to cure them of various unsightly venereal diseases?

PRUDHOE: *(Losing again.)* Fuck it!

SWINTON: No, sir. I am not.

PRUDHOE: Keep 'earin' these screams in me 'ead of all the folks what I've done in, all screamin' and pleadin'.

SWINTON: I live in a nice flat, I drive a nice car, I 'ave a nice missus, I 'ave two well-mannered kids in private schools, we drink nice wine of an evening, and we even, believe it or not, we even once in a while frequent the theatre!

PRUDHOE: Will God ever forgive us, you fink?

SWINTON: I 'ave tax-free money in the bank and, unlike you it seems, me mental equilibrium is not unsettled when I consider some of the bloody deeds what we have 'ad to do for all this material contentment.

PRUDHOE: That's because it's me, not you, what always does the actual murderin'!

SWINTON reveals his cards.

(Knocking over the crate.) Bollocks, bollocks, bollocks!

PAXTON enters, handkerchief to her mouth, shopping bag in the other.

PAXTON: I crack the bones of rats beneath my feet and slip in faecal matter.

SWINTON: The last geezer we brought down 'ere, 'e got the collywobbles.

PAXTON: Could you not open a window?

SWINTON: There *is* no window.

PAXTON: I can scarcely breathe.

SWINTON: We're twenty-five feet below street level.

PAXTON: What's all this goo upon the floor?

SWINTON: You don't wanna know.

PAXTON: I am slipping in goo! I am slipping in slime! I am slipping and sliding in slime and in goo!

SWINTON: We'll give it an 'ose down.

PAXTON: These shoes are appallingly expensive.

SWINTON: My missus would like a pair o' them.

PAXTON: You think so?

SWINTON: You'll have to tell me where you bought 'em.

PAXTON: I shop. I do confess that I shop. I am a shopper. I love to shop. And what I mostly shop for is shoes. I am a shoe shopper. A shopper of shoes. A footwear fanatic. People may look at me and say there goes a woman of the early 1960s, an emancipated woman, no longer subservient to some bullying little male, no longer chained to the kitchen sink, nor endlessly pregnant, with mewling infants forever guzzling at her teats, a woman who is free to earn her own money and yes all this is of course true. And yet, while I celebrate my independence from men, still I value my femininity and therefore what I mostly spend my hard-earned salary on is shoes. A woman can simply never own enough. I am also, it should be said,

33

an ambitious civil servant who must occasionally get her hands dirty helping oil the wheels of the pitiless and patriarchal British Empire. So this then is he?

SWINTON: I do hope so.

PAXTON: What do you mean, you hope so?

SWINTON: Just my little joke.

PAXTON: We really don't have time for jokes.

SWINTON: Pick all my winnings up, will yer!?

PRUDHOE: Bollocks, bollocks, bollocks!

PAXTON: I beg your pardon?

SWINTON: Don't worry about 'im. 'e's just unlucky with 'is cards.

PRUDHOE, on his hands and knees, starts picking up the cards and coins on the floor.

PAXTON: Gambling's a mug's game.

PRUDHOE: Bollocks!

PAXTON: Mr Duns, I do believe?

DUNS responds inaudibly.

PAXTON: I can't quite make out what he's saying?

SWINTON: That's 'cos he's still got a pair of me wife's tights around his mush.

PAXTON: Then perhaps you might remove them?

SWINTON removes the gag as DUNS gasps for breath.

PAXTON: That Sir Nicholas would jeopardise his whole career, his whole life and reputation, for some bare-back rutting with a funny-looking fellow like this...

DUNS: Please, miss!

PAXTON: Now then, Mr Duns, you are it seems placing us in a most unfortunate position. You must realise that?

DUNS: What are you gonna do to me?!

PAXTON: We have been paying you a nice little retainer for the last few years on the understanding that you were to maintain your silence.

DUNS: I just need a bit more, is all.

PAXTON: A bit more?

DUNS: That's right.

PAXTON: I would hardly class a demand for a fifty per cent pay rise as 'a bit more.'

DUNS: I got debts.

SWINTON: Neither a borrower nor a lender be.

PAXTON: Now that's sound advice.

DUNS: I got drug people after me.

PAXTON: We also took your word for it that the photographs you handed over initially, the ones of Sir Nicholas sprawling naked on a bed whilst gripping his rather unremarkable little member, were the only incriminating documents in existence, and that all you still have in your possession are these three sordid love letters he penned but you are now telling us...

DUNS: ...I have a film recording, yes.

PAXTON: And what is this film recording of?

DUNS: It's of me and Sir Nicholas.

PAXTON: You and Sir Nicholas doing what?

DUNS: Me and Sir Nicholas doing it.

PAXTON: And what is the 'it' that you and Sir Nicholas are doing?

DUNS: Well, he's sort of doing *me.*

PAXTON: Doing you?

DUNS: Sort of from behind.

PAXTON: Sort of doing you from behind?

DUNS: While I'm sort of dressed as a baby.

PAXTON: He's sort of doing you from behind while you're sort of dressed as a baby?

DUNS: It's sort of what he likes.

PAXTON: And how did this film recording come into existence?

DUNS: I sort of made it.

PAXTON: You sort of made it?

DUNS: When we first…

PAXTON: Without his prior knowledge?

DUNS: I sort of got a mate to take it from sort of inside a wardrobe.

PAXTON: With the clear intention of blackmailing him later on?

DUNS: Sort of.

PAXTON: Well, I have to tell you that both Sir Nicholas and I are now sort of running out of patience.

DUNS: I just need a bit extra to get these bastards off me back.

PAXTON: We have been paying you a princely salary for over three years now.

DUNS: I got the mind of a child, miss!

PAXTON: You were living on the streets, sir, when Sir
    Nicholas, the bloody idiot, first picked you up and took
    you to his Kensington flat.

DUNS: I just don't know how to handle money!

SWINTON: Bit risky, wannit?

PAXTON: Excuse me?

SWINTON: For a man of his station to take a rent boy back to
    his flat!

PAXTON: Of course it was risky!

SWINTON: No need to shout, love.

PAXTON: Because I'm the one who always has to pick up the
    pieces!

DUNS: Okay, look, forget it. Let's carry on as we were. Let's
    forget I ever asked for more. Just let me go and we can all…

PAXTON: What about this film?

DUNS: I can send you the reel.

PAXTON: How can I be sure you've not made copies?

DUNS: I haven't, I swear!

SWINTON: Can I make a suggestion?

PAXTON: Go on.

SWINTON: Economically speaking this whole arrangement
    don't make much sense.

PAXTON: Go on.

SWINTON: Now I don't know too much about the Ins and
    Outs of this particular affair.

PRUDHOE laughs.

PAXTON: What's so amusing?

PRUDHOE: Well, the Ins and outs!

SWINTON: All I know is you paid us to take 'im from his local and to bring him 'ere.

PAXTON: So?

SWINTON: But it's clear he's got you over a barrel.

PAXTON: I know.

SWINTON: You're payin' 'im for his silence because this Sir Nicholas has a prominent position in the British Establishment...

PAXTON: This we know, this we know!

SWINTON: And the last fing this peer of the realm needs is it to come out he's actually got a penchant for the arses of money-grubbing pooftas like this one here...

PAXTON: Do you possibly have a degree in stating the bleeding obvious?

SWINTON: It'll mean the end of his career.

PAXTON: You don't say!

SWINTON: Not to mention the end of his marriage.

PAXTON: You don't say!

SWINTON: His kids won't respect him.

PAXTON: You don't say!

SWINTON: And, to all intents and purposes, 'is days as a player in this world will be as good as done.

PAXTON: So what do you suggest?

SWINTON: I suggest you just get rid.

PAXTON: Get rid?

DUNS: Wait a minute!

SWINTON: You bike a briefcase with two grand round this afternoon and by the end of the week this luckless character here will be forthwith completely erased from existence.

PAXTON: Are we actually talking murder here?

SWINTON: You can call it what you like.

DUNS: You're gonna *murder* me?

SWINTON: It'll be like he was never even here.

PRUDHOE: Will I be gettin' half of that?

DUNS: Please don't do that?!

SWINTON: If you play your cards right.

PAXTON: I believe I passed a public phone on the way down.

PAXTON leaves.

DUNS: You can't be serious, can you? Guys!? I don't deserve to die, do I? I'm only a kid! I'm only a kid who's fallen on hard times. Who's taken a wrong turn or two! I had a shit childhood! Guys! Guys!

SWINTON: I thought you were gonna clear all this mess up?

PRUDHOE: So I'm really getting a grand?

DUNS: I was a baby when me dad was vaporised at El Alamein.

SWINTON: There's the Queen of Hearts just there, look.

PRUDHOE: I can buy that farmhouse.

DUNS: Me mam sort of lost the plot!

SWINTON: You'll get it only if it's you what does the actual deed.

DUNS: She sort of married a psychopath!

PRUDHOE: It's *always* me!

DUNS: Me stepdad, every day he beat the shit out of me and me sister.

SWINTON: Well, *I* can't kill him as he's just a harmless little twot.

DUNS: He interfered with both of us!

PRUDHOE: So, what, I strangle him and dump in the sea?

DUNS: We told Mum and they threw us both out!

SWINTON: Think we'll go to Scotland again.

DUNS: Me sister hanged herself and I lived on the streets!

PRUDHOE: I like Scotland.

DUNS: I never had a chance!

PRUDHOE: Weigh him down and drop him in a Loch?

SWINTON: Did you know there's more fresh water in Loch Ness than in all the lakes and rivers of England and Wales combined?

DUNS: I been bullied and abused every single day of my life!

PAXTON: *(Returning.)* Okay so I've spoken to Sir Nicholas and he's sending the money over now.

DUNS: Please, let me speak to him!

PAXTON: But you must, he insists, be extremely careful?

SWINTON: As soon as the cash is in my paw his problems will be over.

PAXTON: Okay so…a pleasure doing business with you.

DUNS: Nick promised me he loved me, said he loved me, said he'd always take care of me!

PAXTON: I now intend to take luncheon at Rules with one of my innumerable and, it goes without saying, my extraordinarily wealthy lovers.

PAXTON leaves as SWINTON puts the gag back on DUNS.

SWINTON: What you wanna do while we wait?

PRUDHOE: Another hand?

SWINTON: Might as well.

PRUDHOE: And this time I'm the bank.

SWINTON: Whatever you say, my friend. Whatever you say.

PRUDHOE begins dealing.

III. THE MOTHER OF ALL CONSPIRACY THEORIES

The commandant's dining room in his house by a concentration camp.
A Schubert string quartet plays on throughout. Two couples are eating.
All but LOTTE are fairly drunk. MAX, in a striped uniform, stands
anxiously by.

DIETER: And so?

HEINRICH: This sauce is most interesting.

DIETER: Interesting in a good way?

LOTTE: It's very good, Dieter.

DIETER: Or in a bad way?

HEINRICH: I really cannot decide.

LOTTE: I myself like this flavour very much.

DIETER: Would you, Lotte, care to identify the ingredients?

FRIEDA: Oh, for the love of God!

DIETER: My darling?

FRIEDA: We all *know* it is chicken!

DIETER: The meat is clearly chicken, yes. But our guests are
　　to guess the constituents of the sauce.

FRIEDA: Why does he always have to do this?

DIETER: Why does he always have to do what, oh light of my life?

FRIEDA: He cannot ever play a piece of chamber music
　　on the gramophone but he must always ask our guests
　　'identify the composer' or 'tell me the nationality of the
　　composer' or 'identify the decade in which the music was
　　composed' and he cannot look at a bird in the garden
　　without identifying its species and giving its Latin name
　　and the size and colour of its eggs and…

DIETER: There have been no birds seen around the camp for quite some time now.

FRIEDA: And the clouds are never just clouds, are they, oh no, they must always be either cirrus or scumbulus or stratonumbulus or...

DIETER: Strato*cumulus*, my sweetest.

FRIEDA: And we can never ever eat anything without him forever listing the ingredients...

DIETER: I'm sure our guests would just be interested to know...

FRIEDA: Are we so stuck for conversation?

LOTTE: There is clearly a hint of red wine here?

DIETER: The same red wine we are currently drinking.

FRIEDA: I mean to say, there happens to be a world war raging outside our window.

HEINRICH: I agree this is most excellent.

DIETER: A Château de la Fonveille, 1939.

FRIEDA: We are fighting for our very lives!

HEINRICH: Personally I would never use such a fine wine just for cooking.

DIETER: I have crates of it in the cellar.

LOTTE: Do I also detect honey, apple, garlic, ginger?

DIETER: You do indeed.

FRIEDA: This is a struggle we must on no account lose.

MAX: Do *you* approve of the sauce, sir?

HEINRICH: I'm sorry, is it talking to me?

43

FRIEDA: So perhaps we might find one or two slightly more interesting topics to discuss?

DIETER: This is Max, our chef. He is also our waiter, our cleaner, our toilet attendant.

HEINRICH: That may be so, but why is it addressing me?

DIETER: He is always eager to please.

FRIEDA: The whole of European culture is currently in peril!

HEINRICH: Should I wish to compliment you on your cooking I will do so when I feel like it and not a moment sooner.

MAX: I apologise.

FRIEDA: I for one do not wish to live in a world without National Socialism.

LOTTE: It *is* a very interesting sauce.

FRIEDA: So if we *do* lose this fight then I shall be taking my own life.

DIETER: Please don't be ridiculous.

FRIEDA: I am *not* being ridiculous.

DIETER: We have three children, my precious!

FRIEDA: And I will not, Dieter, have them living in a world run by liberals and Jews!

DIETER: Max, Heinrich, used to be a university lecturer back in the day.

FRIEDA: I will drown them all one by one rather.

DIETER: Was something of an expert on Schopenhauer.

LOTTE: I believe I can taste mustard also?

DIETER: Max sometimes stays up late with me and we chat, do we not?

MAX: We do, sir.

FRIEDA: *(A sudden rage.)* And yes, he would far rather spend his nights conversing with this creature than come to the marital bed with me!

A silence.

LOTTE: It really is most excellent, Max.

FRIEDA: He prefers the company of this filthy Jew to that of his own wife.

DIETER: Max pours me my wine and listens to me pontificate about philosophy.

MAX: You are very knowledgeable, sir.

DIETER: You flatter me.

MAX: Rarely do you, as you say, pontificate.

DIETER: Max was once a lecturer at the university I was hoping to attend before the war.

FRIEDA: Not this again.

DIETER: But then you rejected me, didn't you?

MAX: I was never actually on the Board of Admissions so…

DIETER: They said my essay on Herr Schopenhauer was childish and lacked any real insight.

MAX: I'm sure, sir, that…

DIETER: But now here I am with the life of both him and his family balanced precariously in the palm of my hand.

HEINRICH: We used to have a Jew working as *our* cook.

LOTTE: Well, Max here is clearly a genius with a saucepan.

MAX: Thank you, Madam, for your generous words.

HEINRICH: Do not presume to address my wife in this manner!

MAX: I apologise.

HEINRICH: And step further away from her.

MAX: *(Doing so.)* Of course.

HEINRICH: Don't want you breathing your Jew breath all over her, do we?

LOTTE: Darling, please!

DIETER: So what happened to your cook?

HEINRICH: She was caught stealing cabbages.

DIETER: And so what did you do?

HEINRICH: I had her dragged into the commandant's office and there I interrogated her at length. She was from Budapest, I believe, and had been a famous ballet dancer in her former life. And yes, perhaps, had she not been one of the *Untermensch*, then I might well have found her in some way physically appealing. Her hair was shaved of course but her figure was still full, her legs long and graceful and she possessed the most beguiling pair of brown eyes. She had clearly been a woman of education and culture and previously there had been something disdainful about the way she regarded me, me a mere farmer's boy from Bavaria. But now the mere farmer's boy was to decide her fate. So I told her to dance for me. I told her if she could move me to tears with her dance then perhaps I might let her live. I looked through the commandant's record collection and read out the titles and told her to choose. In a voice shaking with terror she chose. She danced the Dying Swan.

46

The music fades in. A dancer appears and briefly dances.

It *was* rather beautiful, I must confess. I was transported by the way she moved across the floor. I very nearly wept but of course I held myself properly in check. And then… and then she stumbled on her weak legs and she fell at my feet. And there she remained, sobbing and pleading and grovelling and mewling like some animal on the floorboards, kissing my boots and offering me her body in exchange for her life. And so from a thing of beauty all she was to me at that moment was nothing, nothing, nothing at all.

A silence.

LOTTE: What did you do to her?

HEINRICH: Had the bitch hanged by the neck.

LOTTE: Oh, Heinrich, but that's so horrible!

HEINRICH: She performed another kind of dance entirely, jerking and twitching on the end of that rope.

A silence.

FRIEDA: My husband of course would have behaved differently had she made the same offer to *him* since, oh, how he likes to leave our bed, if ever he deigns come to it, to go prowling the camp in search of….

DIETER: Enough!

A silence.

My wife, as you know, suffers from these dark moods and so…

FRIEDA: Your wife suffers from nothing save having a husband who no longer loves her!

A long silence.

47

DIETER: Well, Max wouldn't ever steal from us.

FRIEDA: You say that but...

DIETER: Would you, Max?

MAX: Of course not, sir.

FRIEDA: Because now I come to think of it...

DIETER: He has his wife and his poor old parents depending on him here.

FRIEDA: I am currently missing some jewellery.

MAX: Jewellery, Madam?

FRIEDA: I cannot locate that necklace your parents gave me for Christmas.

DIETER: Max is not a thief.

MAX: Absolutely not, sir.

DIETER: I have always been very good to you, have I not?

MAX: You have always been very good to me.

FRIEDA: I want you to search him, Dieter.

DIETER: And how long has it been now?

MAX: Just over a year.

FRIEDA: Did you hear what I said?

DIETER: You see, he and his wife and parents, they have been placed in slightly nicer accommodation than the rest of them, have you not?

MAX: We are much more comfortable where we are, sir.

FRIEDA: I want you to search him right now.

DIETER: His father helps with the burning of the bodies.

MAX: He does, sir.

FRIEDA: I would do it myself but these people are always crawling with...

DIETER: And is he happy in his work, do you know?

MAX: That I couldn't say.

DIETER: Well, surely you must talk together?

MAX: I didn't steal your wife's pearls, sir.

DIETER: I am quite certain you did not.

MAX: Thank you, sir.

DIETER: For you are a highly intelligent man, are you not?

MAX: I don't know, sir.

DIETER: And stealing even a slice of bread from us would mean instant liquidation, would it not?

MAX: I am sure it would, sir.

FRIEDA: Wait a moment, please!

DIETER: Darling?

FRIEDA: How did he know my necklace was made of pearls?

MAX: I think I've...I've seen you wear it?

FRIEDA: I *rarely* wear it.

DIETER: You *often* wear it.

MAX: I'm sure then, Madam, that I must have noticed it...

FRIEDA: I keep it in my dressing table drawer.

MAX: Please believe me...

FRIEDA: I did take it out to try on one day last week so thought perhaps I'd left it out but…

MAX: I swear to you…

FRIEDA: Search him, Dieter.

DIETER: This man is a Doctor of Philosophy, darling…

FRIEDA: Then I shall do it myself.

DIETER: You'd better remove your clothing, Max old boy.

MAX: I swear on the life of my wife and my mother that…

FRIEDA: Remove your jacket.

MAX removes his jacket.

Now pass it to me.

MAX: *(Passing it to her.)* I've never stolen anything before in my life.

FRIEDA: This clothing absolutely reeks.

She turns out the pockets. Hurls his various tragic little items on the ground.

HEINRICH: How the mighty have fallen.

DIETER: He certainly doesn't look like a Doctor of Philosophy now.

FRIEDA: And now the shirt.

MAX: You want me to remove it?

LOTTE: Is all this absolutely necessary?

FRIEDA: See what you're hiding under there.

MAX starts unbuttoning his shirt.

DIETER: Come on then. Tell my unenlightened friends here about Schopenhauer. Show them how 'childish and lacking in real insight' is *my* understanding by comparison.

MAX: You must forgive me but...

DIETER: Just do it!

MAX: Well, his basic argument is that there are two fundamental ways of looking at the world.

FRIEDA: Now pass it to me.

MAX: *(Passing her the shirt.)* There is the world as will, which is the ultimate thing in itself, which is independent of the human mind.

HEINRICH: He looks very well-fed to *me.*

MAX: And there is the world as representation, as it is perceived by us through our human senses.

FRIEDA: I was going to say the same.

HEINRICH: Most of the other inmates here are largely skin and bone.

DIETER: Impress us further with your capacious intellect.

MAX: Representations are constructed by the mind according to its conditioning forms of space, time and causality; they are the objects which are individuated, or picked out, by the human mind.

DIETER: Are you lot listening to this?

FRIEDA: And now for the trousers.

MAX: Madam, this is most humiliating.

DIETER: You might just learn something.

FRIEDA: There's just something about you convinces me you have my necklace.

MAX: Please, sir, may this stop, please.

DIETER: I outlined all these things in my essay but still I was rejected.

MAX: For that I am sorry.

DIETER: You think I would have made a good student there?

MAX: I'm sure you would have, sir!

DIETER: Then why in God's name, man, did you ever turn me down!?

FRIEDA holds up a pearl necklace.

MAX: I swear to God, sir, I didn't take it.

FRIEDA: Guilty as charged.

DIETER: Now then, this is a pity!

MAX: Please believe me.

FRIEDA: You need to take him outside and shoot him this instant.

LOTTE: Forgive me, but you were showing me this necklace before we sat down to supper.

FRIEDA: I have a very similar one.

LOTTE: It was identical to that one.

FRIEDA: It is similar, that is all.

MAX: Sir, I beg you!

LOTTE: She has just now planted it on the poor man!

DIETER: Kindly do not infer that my wife would do such a thing?

HEINRICH: Kindly do not infer that my wife would infer such a thing!

LOTTE: I am not inferring it, I am stating it as a fact!

FRIEDA: You must now punish this man, Dieter.

DIETER thinks for a time, then rises unsteadily from the table.

DIETER: Tell me, Max, have you enjoyed serving me and my family for the last year?

MAX: It has been a pleasure to serve you, sir.

DIETER: Don't lie to me.

MAX: This wasn't a lie.

DIETER: You hate us all with every bone in your body.

MAX: I really didn't take the necklace!

DIETER: If you could you'd take this gun and blow my brains out, wouldn't you?

MAX: Nothing could be further from the truth, sir.

DIETER: Here.

FRIEDA: Oh God, he's so drunk again.

DIETER: Take the gun.

FRIEDA: Drunk before we've even finished the main bloody course!

DIETER holds out his pistol towards MAX.

DIETER: Take it.

FRIEDA: Lotte, this man starts on the wine almost as soon as he wakes up.

HEINRICH: Do not give your Jew the pistol.

LOTTE: I think clearly that the pressure of work might sometimes make our men…

DIETER: Take it and blow out my brains.

MAX: I'm not going to do that, sir.

DIETER: And then afterwards you can blow out my wife's brains and the brains of my dreadful friends here.

FRIEDA: Ridding the world of the Jewish pestilence is the most noble endeavour in the history of mankind.

LOTTE: Is that *really* what we are doing?

FRIEDA: And one cannot make an omelette, can one, without first breaking one or two eggs?

DIETER: Take the pistol, Max!

MAX: I cannot.

DIETER: This is a direct order!

MAX hesitantly takes the pistol.

This man here is the only semi-intelligent being in this whole godforsaken place.

MAX: That isn't at all true, sir.

DIETER: Now point it at my head!

LOTTE: I'm leaving now if this stupidity continues!

HEINRICH: If you raise that gun an inch higher than you have it now then…

DIETER: Do it!

HEINRICH: …I will put a bullet through your heart before you can say…

DIETER: Do it now, Max!

HEINRICH: …Yom kippur!

A long silence.

DIETER: *(Quiet, serious.)* Just do it.

MAX: But this will mean *my* death, the death of my wife and the death of my parents.

FRIEDA: You see how this man actually loves *his* wife, Dieter!?

DIETER: You have stolen from my sweet Frieda.

MAX: No!

DIETER: So whatever happens your own extinction is absolutely guaranteed.

MAX: Please.

DIETER: But the war is over. The Allies are advancing from the west, the Russians from the east. We will not retreat. We must die here like true Germans.

LOTTE: This is madness, Dieter!

MAX: How can I save my family?

DIETER: No one can now be saved.

MAX: No one?

DIETER: But surely you would like to take one or two of us down with you?

MAX quickly raises the pistol. As soon as he does so HEINRICH fires his at him, but misses. Fires again, misses. The third time he is out of bullets.

HEINRICH: *Scheisse!*

DIETER: *(Laughing.)* You are even drunker than I, Heinrich!

MAX aims his pistol at the Germans, slowly moving his aim around from one to the other.

FRIEDA: Put that gun down.

DIETER: Please: kill my appalling wife first. I'd so love to see the bitch bleed out, twitching and howling there on her new Afghan rug!

FRIEDA now approaches the semi-naked man, whose pistol points at her.

FRIEDA: You will hand me that pistol this instant, Jew, and then you will do my bidding.

HEINRICH: *(Standing.)* A new world order is coming, you understand?

FRIEDA: Your people have controlled everything for too long and now the tide has finally turned.

HEINRICH: We *will* have our Utopia, Jew.

FRIEDA: We will have it and we will have it soon.

HEINRICH: And we will have it for a thousand years.

FRIEDA: And to build any Utopia it will always be a fight to the death.

HEINRICH: And because you betrayed us to the Russians in the last war we had to suffer twenty years of poverty, of misery, you understand?

MAX: But I fought in the trenches as a loyal German!

HEINRICH: We know what it's like to be starving.

FRIEDA: We had to make soup from our leather belts.

HEINRICH: We ate nettles and grass.

FRIEDA: As a girl I smashed in the skull of my best friend with a brick as we scrapped over a single apple core.

HEINRICH: We even butchered the family cat and took turns gnawing on her bones.

FRIEDA: I vowed to myself and to my children that in the name of God we would never ever go hungry again!

HEINRICH: And were we not here exterminating the Jew, the gypsy, the communist and the queer then, you know it yourself, you would all of you ensure the pure-blooded Anglo-Saxon race is wiped from the face of this earth.

FRIEDA: The survival of the fittest, yes?

HEINRICH: The natural order of things.

FRIEDA: Either kill or be killed.

DIETER: You really should have married Heinrich, my darling. You two would have made such a delightful couple.

FRIEDA: Now I order you to put down that gun!

MAX shoots FRIEDA at point-blank range and she drops.

DIETER: Excellent, Max! The way you have countered their arguments is worthy of a professor of…

MAX shoots DIETER and he drops. He now aims at HEINRICH.

HEINRICH: Wait, Jew. Let me first take a moment to prepare myself for…

MAX shoots him and he drops. He now aims the pistol at LOTTE.

LOTTE: I am just an ordinary woman. An ordinary mother. My only crime is not to have asked enough questions. My husband went out to work and he took care of us so well and so I asked nothing. I was ignorant, Max. Unforgivably, stupidly ignorant. My head has been for too long in the sand. But you know I am not a wicked woman. I am not like all these others. I have only recently learned what my people are doing to your people. And it sickens me, Max, please believe me. I have two innocent children who need me and so, listen, perhaps I could find some way to help you and your family escape from here and the way you are looking at me is making me extremely frightened and just now, you may recall, I was the one who complimented you on your sauce…

MAX: You separated us from *our* innocent children, Lotte. My baby girl was snatched away from her mother's arms.

LOTTE: But not I, Max!

MAX: Little Edie was screaming so loudly a soldier simply shot her though her head right before our eyes. And she lay there in the snow suddenly so still, suddenly so silent. Oscar and Anne were clinging to our legs before they too were pulled off us and, oh, the sound of a thousand pleading mothers and a thousand sobbing children….

LOTTE: I can help you.

MAX: My poor wife on her knees calling their names until her voice gave out and me powerless to stop any of this happening…

The sounds of many children screaming Mummy, Mummy, Mummy!

I still hear these children crying out to their mothers every moment of every day…

LOTTE: Is there nothing I can do that might save me? In Berlin I was a nurse, Max. My duty was always to ease the suffering of others. Is there no hope at all for me?

MAX: All the ecstasy, all the peace in this life, it comes from within us, Lotte. When all hope seems lost, when the unspeakable has happened, when we are beaten and starved, when we are tortured and murdered, when those we love are slaughtered right in front of us, we can still look inside ourselves, into the stillness and into the emptiness which lies within us all, and there we can always find the seeds of hope. There, in the silence, and if we choose to, we will always hear the gentle and forgiving voice of God.

LOTTE: Oh, Max, Max, God bless your humanity. God bless you for your infinite...

MAX shoots her.

...mercy.

She drops and is still.

The sound of aircraft overhead, explosions. Boots marching, Russian singing.

He drops the gun.

IV. OLD MEN TALKING, YOUNG MEN DYING

A brothel a few miles from the front line. BEATRICE is singing. When she finishes the song there is a scattered round of applause. Distant explosions throughout.

JULIET: You have such a voice.

BEATRICE: Thank you.

JULIET: But, oh, it is so sad how thin you are becoming.

BEATRICE: All I think about these days is food.

JULIET: So do as I suggest and you'll be able to afford some bread and cheese for your supper tonight.

BEATRICE: I cannot do it.

JULIET: The world has gone to hell, my dear.

BEATRICE: I know but…

JULIET: No longer can we maintain the lofty moral standards of peacetime.

BEATRICE: There must be another way?

JULIET: Tell me it.

BEATRICE: The world may have gone to hell but I do not wish to go there.

JULIET: God will forgive you.

BEATRICE: Are you sure?

JULIET: He wants you to survive.

BEATRICE: Even at the expense of my immortal soul?

JULIET: That is why He's given you such beautiful, kissable lips, my dear.

FRANK: She is a woman, that's all. Not some Hun with a hand grenade.

ARTHUR: I can't wait, Sarge.

FRANK: Do me a favour, look at you. You're terrified. I seen you shittin' yourself less waitin' to go over the top.

ARTHUR: Leave it out.

FRANK: She'll do some amazing things to you.

ARTHUR: Right.

FRANK: Make you feel like you've died and gone to heaven.

ARTHUR: I've never even kissed a girl before.

FRANK: My Juliet is finding someone extra special for you. And she knows this'll be your very first time.

*

BEATRICE: All I want is to sing.

JULIET: *I* wanted to sing once upon a time.

BEATRICE: Singing is what God put me on this earth to do.

JULIET: We all of us wanted to sing, my little nightingale.

BEATRICE: When I sing it's as if I myself am no longer present. It is like some higher power is directing me.

JULIET: That's a lovely thought.

BEATRICE: And if I cannot sing then I could be a nurse perhaps?

JULIET: Nursing or whoring or manufacturing bombs...

BEATRICE: But where do I go...

JULIET: …that's all that is open to a woman in wartime.

BEATRICE: …when I have an elderly mother who needs me here?

JULIET: All occupations the consequence of male restlessness.

BEATRICE: A mother who is starving.

JULIET: You suck the cock of some English soldier…

BEATRICE: Please do not even say the words…

JULIET: …then you go home and you spoil her with some half-decent grub.

BEATRICE: I feel sick you even say it.

JULIET: Put a nice big smile on the old lady's face.

BEATRICE: When will men on this earth stop killing one another?

JULIET: I was proud of my husband when he first put on his uniform.

BEATRICE: While I urged my brothers to flee abroad.

JULIET: You'd have them live as cowards in another country?

BEATRICE: No. I would simply have them *live*.

*

FRANK: We really gotta live in this moment, you understand?

ARTHUR: I think so.

FRANK: Really experience every single second. Fill up your senses with the here and now. No matter how ordinary it seems on the surface of things. The moonlight comin' in through that window, the smell of the damp air, the taste of your beer. Really savour every sip of it. Feel the breath in our bodies, the blood flowin' through our veins. See,

I realise now that this moment, *this* moment, Arthur, this moment here, and this one and this one, this is all there ever is. You get me? And maybe if we all stopped trying to be somewhere else, if we all stopped wanting more than what there is, if we just stayed where we are and delighted in it all, then we might not be here now blowing the shit out of each other.

ARTHUR: Never heard you talk like this, Sarge?

FRANK: It's 'cos I know in me bones we're all gonna cop it tomorrow. You and me, the rest of the boys: I tell yer… this is our final night on this planet.

ARTHUR: How you so certain?

FRANK: 'Cos I been told. The mission we're on. Drawing enemy fire. We're a diversion. Mate overheard the top brass callin' it a suicide attack. We're bein' sacrificed so the enemy don't concentrate on the main attack from the rear.

ARTHUR: I don't understand.

FRANK: We got no supportin' fire, Arthur, no air cover, no nothin'. They're gonna cut us all down like cattle. Were I a gamblin' man I'd put money on it not one of us'll come out of it alive.

ARTHUR: Dear God…

FRANK: That's why we gotta get your poor little cherry popped tonight.

*

JULIET: Don't cry, my love.

BEATRICE: I cannot do this.

JULIET: Course you can.

BEATRICE: I have never ever been with a man.

JULIET: You know how many bits of men lie rotting outside
this room, fertilising our once-peaceful French fields?
How many bits of Germans, how many bits of British,
how many bits of our own boys? How many tons of
human flesh are right now rotting into the earth? So many
boys, so many beautiful boys. Every one of them his
mother's pride and joy. All with childhoods in the sun and
great hopes for their days to come. And not one of them
will ever be seen on this earth again. Only, when future
summers warm the land and poppies grow where once
they fell, only then might they hopefully be remembered.
And so you, you must forget all about your immortal soul.
You must open your legs for some horny English boy who
himself is destined to die, you must grit your teeth and
think on other things and then you must take his grubby
money in your hand and you must survive. You must
ensure that you, and those you love, you must ensure you
live, you survive. And then afterwards that you prosper.

*

FRANK: How you doin', darlin'?

JULIET: All the better for seeing you, Frank.

FRANK: This is Arthur. The innocent lamb I was telling you
about.

JULIET: Hello, Arthur.

FRANK: He's very shy with the ladies.

JULIET: No need to be shy with us. You're amongst friends
now.

FRANK: I seen him screamin' like a banshee across No Man's
Land, seen him skewerin' a man with a bayonet, seen
him spillin' a German's guts out onto the mud but, I tell

yer, leadin' him to you tonight's been like leadin' a man towards a firin' squad.

ARTHUR: He's exaggerating.

JULIET: I'm not listening to him, don't worry.

FRANK: I'm serious!

JULIET: And this is Beatrice.

ARTHUR: Nice to meet you.

JULIET: We call her our little nightingale.

FRANK: I've heard you sing here many time, miss.

JULIET: She sings like an angel.

FRANK: You have a very lovely voice.

BEATRICE: Thank you, sir.

JULIET: These two brave men are risking their lives for the freedom of France.

BEATRICE: Thank you for protecting our country.

ARTHUR: I don't actually agree with that.

FRANK: You don't agree with what?

ARTHUR: That we're fighting for the freedom of France. That we're fighting for freedom at all.

FRANK: What the hell *else* are we doing?

ARTHUR: I dunno but we're not doing that.

JULIET: This *is* what you are doing, Arthur. You are stopping this huge German monster from devouring all of Europe so…

ARTHUR: But there is surely no German monster and no British monster. There is only the monster of Empire.

65

There is the French Empire alongside the British Empire, that have both been raping and pillaging the globe for the last three hundred years or so and now there is this new German Empire rising from its slumbers and daring to challenge them.

FRANK: That just now is the longest I've ever heard him speak.

JULIET: You some kind of Bolshevik, Arthur?

ARTHUR: We're not fighting for anything noble. It's just these rapacious empires, locking horns over who's to control the world's resources, the world's markets. It's a great crime the governing classes of Europe are perpetrating on their own people.

JULIET: Come on, who wants a beer?

FRANK: I do.

ARTHUR: And, yes, I think maybe these Russians have got it right.

JULIET fetches bottles.

JULIET: German militarism must be stopped, Arthur.

ARTHUR: What quarrel do we have with the working classes of any country? These German boys we're fighting and killing are our brothers. Every single soldier out here on all sides, French, German, British, American…we should all turn around right now, go home and shoot all the cigar smokers, the port swillers, all the fat old men with their big moustaches who've sent us here to die, the ones who stand to make a fortune from the slaughter.

FRANK: He reads too much.

BEATRICE: So why don't you do it?

FRANK: Nose forever in some book or another.

BEATRICE: Why don't you turn round, go home and shoot all the politicians and the businessmen?

ARTHUR: I don't know.

FRANK: I have to be honest with you though: I've bloody loved this war. Never felt so alive. Never felt so part of things. Course there's been horrible days and there's been blood and guts and death but somehow I feel as if I been privileged in a way. I made the best mates here I've ever known. I've known and loved some really great fellas. Like being part of one big family. 'Cos I've never known family, me. I seen the love that exists between men. And the courage. And, yes, noble things, Arthur. You know? My life before was dull, dull, dull. No job, no money, no sense of security. And I was always so lonely. So cut off. It was like Hell. A hell in a way that was worse than this. 'Cos this, this is big. And the way people live in peacetime, it's just buying and selling and struggling and getting on, everyone on the make all the time. At least the work out here is honest work. And if we die, so what? We're dying for something important, something bigger than ourselves. We're young and we're brave and we're dying for our country. Not just falling to pieces from some stupid disease when we're old and helpless and soft in the head. And the exhilaration I feel on the field of battle, when death is everywhere, when you're so alert, so aware, each moment so intense and so precious and so exciting, when any moment you could be blown to pieces, well, it just all seems so beautiful somehow. It's like a kind of ecstasy. I dunno what I'm trying to say really. *(A pause.)* Anyway we're both gonna be dead by this time tomorrow so…

JULIET: You don't know that?

FRANK: *(Serious.)* Believe me, my love. I do know.

ARTHUR: I signed up 'cos I wanted my dad to take some notice of me, to be proud of me.

JULIET: I'm sure he *is* proud.

FRANK: Come on, love. I've one night remaining to me in this life and it's my honour to be spending it with you.

JULIET: That's kind of beautiful, Frank.

FRANK: Don't wanna listen to no more politics.

JULIET: Let's leave these lovebirds to it.

JULIET and FRANK leave.

BEATRICE: Your beer?

ARTHUR: Thank you.

She passes him a bottle.

I'm afraid I've never done this before.

BEATRICE: Nor I.

ARTHUR: I see.

A silence.

Are you not drinking?

BEATRICE: No, thank you.

A silence.

I'm told I must ask for payment in advance.

ARTHUR: Yes. Sorry. Of course.

He hands her some banknotes.

Is that the correct amount?

BEATRICE: I think so. Thank you.

A silence.

Are you alright? You seem a little…

ARTHUR: It feels like for a year now…

BEATRICE: …tearful.

ARTHUR: …I've been living in a nightmare I can't wake up from.

BEATRICE: I understand.

ARTHUR: The things I've seen. The things I've done.

BEATRICE: And are you really going to die tomorrow?

ARTHUR drinks her in for a time.

What are you doing?

ARTHUR: Something the Sarge said. He said this moment now is all there ever is. And we should appreciate the beautiful things around us. While we still can.

BEATRICE: That is of course true.

ARTHUR: And you, Beatrice, are a very beautiful thing.

BEATRICE: Thank you.

ARTHUR: And it makes me feel very sad that you must work in a place like this.

BEATRICE: What about you? You seem so bright, so full of ideas.

ARTHUR: There are many men much brighter than me dying every day out there.

A silence.

BEATRICE: So…

ARTHUR: So…

BEATRICE: Shall we get this thing done?

Hesitantly she starts to unbutton her blouse.

*

JULIET and FRANK having noisy, rough sex. He is trying to kiss her but each time she turns her face away from him. He finishes. He starts dressing.

JULIET: Don't stop! Why are you stopping?

FRANK: I wanted to kiss you.

JULIET: You know I never kiss.

FRANK: But this time…

JULIET: I save my kisses for my husband.

FRANK: I so need to…what's the word?

JULIET: So come back to bed!

FRANK: …connect.

JULIET: I thought we were spending this night together?

FRANK: You get off home to your husband. Tell him he's a very lucky man.

JULIET: A German shell blew off his legs! A German shell completely unmanned him.

FRANK: Is Arthur right, you think? Is it all completely meaningless? Are we just throwing our lives away so those pen pushers, those paper shufflers back home, so they can get all richer and richer?

JULIET: If you do not return, Frank, please know that your sacrifice will not have been in vain. The future of the world is at stake.

FRANK: I long ago made my peace with death so…

JULIET: And you *will* be remembered.

She goes to him, kisses him.

FRANK: Thanks for that.

JULIET: No. Thank *you.*

*

ARTHUR: Stop.

BEATRICE: You want me to stop?

ARTHUR: We don't need to do this.

BEATRICE: *(Stops undressing.)* No?

ARTHUR: You are so lovely and so pure and I think wherever
    we find loveliness and purity we should do all we can to
    honour it. Not turn it corrupt and wicked and foul.

BEATRICE: You don't want to…? You know?

ARTHUR: I want nothing more than to…you know.

BEATRICE: Then we must?

ARTHUR: No.

She offers to return the money.

Keep it. I'm not going to need money after tonight. *(Hands
    her more notes.)* And take this too. This is all I have. It will
    maybe tide you over until all this is over.

BEATRICE: But it's a lot? You don't know for certain you will
    die? Is there nothing at all I can do in return?

ARTHUR: You could maybe sing something?

BEATRICE: What would you like me to sing?

ARTHUR: Something old. Something old and from another world.

BEATRICE now sings.

ARTHUR eventually sobs like a child as her song is drowned out by the sound of explosions.

BEATRICE: *Plaisir d'amour ne dure qu'un moment,*
Chagrin d'amour dure toute la vie.
J'ai tout quitté
Pour l'ingrate Sylvie.
Elle me quitte et prend un autre amant.
Plaisir d'amour ne dure qu'un moment,
Chagrin d'amour dure toute la vie.
'Tant que cette eau coulera doucement
Vers ce ruisseau qui borde la prairie,
Je t'aimerai', me répétait Sylvie.
L'eau coule encor,
Elle a changé pourtant.
Plaisir d'amour ne dure qu'un moment,
Chagrin d'amour dure toute la vie.

V. POINTING TOWARDS THE FUTURE

ANNA-MARIE is putting the finishing touches to her large clay model of LUDWIG, who stands in a heroic pose, pointing into the distance, naked from the waist up. Outside and throughout a large celebratory crowd is chanting his name.

ANNA-MARIE: If you could please keep your arm in that positon, sir?

LUDWIG: How much longer is this likely to take?

ANNA-MARIE: Not long.

LUDWIG: I've been standing like this for two hours now.

ANNA-MARIE: You are pointing towards the future.

LUDWIG: So you keep saying.

ANNA-MARIE: And this statue will stand sentinel guarding the city gates for a thousand years.

LUDWIG: Perhaps a tad optimistic.

ANNA-MARIE: So we need, sir, for it to be exactly right.

LUDWIG: I have spent many long, lonely hours in shell holes and in trenches but this, this is quite purgatorial…

ANNA-MARIE: If you could please…

He lifts his arm back up.

Thank you, sir.

LUDWIG: Tell me you at least have my face by now?

ANNA-MARIE: I do.

LUDWIG: So why can't we get someone else to stand in for my body?

ANNA-MARIE: Because I believe in authenticity.

LUDWIG: I utterly abhor this new-found…what is that word they use with such gay abandon these days?

ANNA-MARIE: Celebrity?

LUDWIG: Yes.

ANNA-MARIE: I am the greatest sculptor in the city and yet I have always found myself…

LUDWIG: I've never heard of you.

ANNA-MARIE: Perhaps then the second greatest.

LUDWIG: So who's the greatest?

ANNA-MARIE: Schwanz.

LUDWIG: Never heard of him either.

ANNA-MARIE: Her.

LUDWIG: Never heard of her.

ANNA-MARIE: Nobody has.

LUDWIG: But she is the greatest?

ANNA-MARIE: And it is of course common that the greatest artist in any field should for their whole lifetime remain painfully obscure.

LUDWIG: Is obscurity always painful?

ANNA-MARIE: If one craves its opposite, yes.

LUDWIG: And what is its opposite?

ANNA-MARIE: I don't know…recognition?

LUDWIG: And do you crave recognition?

ANNA-MARIE: All artists do.

LUDWIG: Which seems to me infantile in the extreme.

ANNA-MARIE: We seek the love and approval denied to us as children.

LUDWIG: Yes. Infantile, as I said.

ANNA-MARIE: I would say that the more well-known and wealthy an artist is, the more you can be sure their work lacks originality, the more they will simply be prostituting their talents to appease the rich and powerful.

LUDWIG: And yet you have a commission from the Emperor!?

ANNA-MARIE: An artist is no longer an artist when he or she stoops for honours from...

LUDWIG: I repeat: you have a commission from the Emperor!

ANNA-MARIE: Only because I have promised to sleep with his dreadful, lisping, predatory son.

LUDWIG: You've had carnal relations with that buffoon!?

ANNA-MARIE: I have *promised* merely.

LUDWIG: The same Prince Otto who's marrying his fiancée next week?

ANNA-MARIE: Which I am hoping will distract him from calling in the favour.

LUDWIG: At massive public expense.

ANNA-MARIE: Sadly the prince is now in charge of all artistic commissions in the capital.

LUDWIG: I am appalled.

ANNA-MARIE: It was the only way I could secure such a life-changing engagement.

LUDWIG: I am utterly disgusted.

ANNA-MARIE: So then it's true what they say?

LUDWIG: What do they say?

ANNA-MARIE: That the sexual act repulses you? That you, who could have any woman you choose in this city, in this entire country in fact, you would rather spend your time walking your dogs or polishing your insanely large collection of expensive leather boots?

LUDWIG: I happen to like my boots.

She works on in silence.

ANNA-MARIE: And for your information: I myself am a proud virgin and I intend to die as one.

LUDWIG: You do?

ANNA-MARIE: *(A sudden rage.)* I will never ever allow my destiny to be shaped by any man!

A silence.

LUDWIG: Go on.

ANNA-MARIE: My dear mother, like her three sisters before her, was traded by her father like livestock to the highest bidder. She spent the rest of her days, almost as soon as her first period came, producing child after child after child, and barely was her umbilical cord cut then was her belly once more swelling with my father's ever-eager seed until her body, her poor abused body, became like a wrinkled, grey sack and her life ended, spent, unhappy and unlived before she even reached the age of thirty. *(A pause.)* If you don't mind me saying so…

LUDWIG: Yes?

ANNA-MARIE: You have a strangely unimpressive physique.
    Your arms don't look as if they could hold up a sword,
    rifle or crossbow.

LUDWIG: I have murdered many with these arms.

ANNA-MARIE: In wartime it is surely not called murder?

LUDWIG: I call it what it is.

ANNA-MARIE: So, although I know there are thousands of
    women out there, below this window, who would gladly
    part their legs for you, probably with the full endorsement
    of their menfolk, those of them who still *have* menfolk of
    course, or menfolk at least with the same number of limbs
    they were born with…

LUDWIG: And now here comes the insult.

ANNA-MARIE: I myself find your features rather unappealing.

LUDWIG: Really?

ANNA-MARIE: I would hesitate to say that you are ugly.

LUDWIG: But the thing is: you are not remotely hesitating?

ANNA-MARIE: But I can, if you like, transform a slight
    ugliness into a…

LUDWIG: So I'm only *slightly* ugly now?

ANNA-MARIE: To have, in your own words, murdered so
    many and yet to be so thin-skinned!

LUDWIG: Since the day of the surrender I have known little
    else but flattery and fawning. I have been received in every
    drawing room of every bewigged dignitary in this city.
    There have been endless puff pastries and endless goblets
    of sweet white wine proffered up by endless genuflecting
    servants on endless silver platters. I have shaken hands with,

and nodded my head at, every official and every minor
aristocrat in the country. I have plastered on a fake smile
as every perfumed old bitch and every insincere careerist
gush forth their gratitude and offer me their hospitality and
their friendship. And now I am compelled by the Crown
Prince to pose for a new statue in bronze, to stand thirty
feet tall on the city gates, a statue being paid for by taxes a
starving population can ill afford to spare and as I stand here
pointing towards the future with an aching arm and sweat
pouring off my skin it seems I have to endure being slighted
by the self-styled second greatest sculptor in the land.

ANNA-MARIE: It was meant as a statement of fact rather than
a slight.

LUDWIG: Therefore I cannot be so thin-skinned?

ANNA-MARIE: No?

LUDWIG: Since I found your insult refreshing.

ANNA-MARIE: I'm an artist. I always tell the truth.

LUDWIG: Is that right?.

ANNA-MARIE: We show mankind as he is.

LUDWIG: You mean, like a mirror?

ANNA-MARIE: Yes, we hold up a mirror, et cetera, et cetera.

LUDWIG: In any real sense how does a mirror tell the truth?

ANNA-MARIE: I hadn't thought.

LUDWIG: When we look into a mirror we merely see the
reflections of our faces, do we not? We see those external
features our parents unthinkingly bestowed upon us in
those desperate moments when, stripped naked and
grunting like hogs in the sty, they rubbed themselves upon
one another in a frenzy of swinish lust. We never in the

glass see the black, hideous reality of our own quaking, wretched, hate-filled souls.

ANNA-MARIE: You don't like yourself very much, do you?

LUDWIG: And anyway you've just stated you are prepared to distort the mirror in order to make me seem slightly less ugly for posterity?

ANNA-MARIE: That's because you saved us all from extermination.

LUDWIG: I've postponed it rather.

ANNA-MARIE: You think our defeat inevitable?

LUDWIG: And possibly desirable.

ANNA-MARIE: In what way desirable?

LUDWIG: Many crimes have been committed for many years by the Emperor and his incestuous line.

ANNA-MARIE: And have *you* committed many crimes?

LUDWIG: They are dancing and singing out there upon the bones of the innocent.

ANNA-MARIE: Have you?

LUDWIG: Let me put it this way: I would never avail myself of all the female flesh you say is on offer out there.

ANNA-MARIE: Why not?

LUDWIG: Because I find a woman's very willingness entirely uninviting.

ANNA-MARIE: I don't understand.

LUDWIG: What I prefer is…

ANNA-MARIE: Yes…?

LUDWIG: To take her by force.

ANNA-MARIE: *(After a pause.)* I see.

LUDWIG: An activity in which, as we pushed the enemy back to their slums and to their shanties, I was able to indulge to my heart's content.

ANNA-MARIE: You have lowered your arm again.

LUDWIG: I see I have unsettled you.

ANNA-MARIE: Not at all.

LUDWIG: Your hand is shaking?

ANNA-MARIE: It's cold in the room.

LUDWIG: On the contrary: it's the height of summer.

ANNA-MARIE: So it is.

LUDWIG: Can you not hear the flies battering their heads against the window panes?

They listen to the buzzing of several flies.

ANNA-MARIE: Now you mention it...

LUDWIG: The sound of flies means more to a soldier than it does to a civilian, you understand?

ANNA-MARIE: Your arm, please?

LUDWIG: The sound of bluebottles buzzing about the naked, slowly decaying corpses of the freshly slaughtered is one of the many I can never quite escape.

ANNA-MARIE: I am now padding out the biceps and the triceps.

LUDWIG: And kindly do not forget to overlook the paunch.

ANNA-MARIE: Consider it overlooked.

LUDWIG: If I am to stand guarding the gates of this city for a thousand years I do not wish future generations to think I had in any way let myself go.

ANNA-MARIE: The Crown Prince Otto wants you to be an immortal symbol.

LUDWIG: And immortal symbols must of course possess neither paunches nor puny arms.

Enter OTTO and LARA.

OTTO: Talking about me, weren't you? What were you saying? Did you hear that, darling? People always talk about me behind my back and one can be quite confident that nothing of what they say is ever terribly nice.

LUDWIG: *(To ANNA-MARIE.)* It is only when a woman hates me and would rather see me dead that my loins begin to twinge. I seek physical intimacy with my enemies alone.

OTTO: You just said I had a paunch and puny arms.

LUDWIG: I was talking about myself.

OTTO: A likely story!

ANNA-MARIE: *(To LUDWIG.)* But I do not hate you?

LUDWIG: Oh, of course you do.

CROWD: *(Off.) We want Ludwig, we want Ludwig!*

OTTO: I have never been a popular prince, have I? Never been what one might call a man of the people. On the few occasions I *have* shown my face amongst my subjects, or my subjects-to-be, as it were, it's not the flag-waving and the cheering I remember, because they don't really love *me*, do they, they only love what I *represent*, that is to say the stability, the history, the endless bloody ceremonies, the very expensive clothing…No, what I *do* remember are the lone voices of 'parasite' and 'inbreed' and 'you'll be the first against the wall, fella'!

LARA: Oh, I am so tired of the sound of your voice.

OTTO: Please don't be cross with me again, my darling.

LARA: All your prattling insecurities.

OTTO: I don't mean to aggravate you.

LARA: You've been aggravating me since the day I first stepped off the boat.

OTTO: General, have you met my betrothed?

LUDWIG: Not officially.

OTTO: This is the Princess Lara…

LUDWIG: But I have on several occasions undressed her with my eyes.

OTTO: Now, there's really no need for that.

Two conversations now separate.

LARA: So how does it feel, General, to be a national hero at such a tender age?

LUDWIG: I'm not really enjoying it.

OTTO: So how's it coming along, oh talented one?

ANNA-MARIE: *You* tell *me.*

LARA: I've been very excited at the prospect of meeting you.

LUDWIG: Anonymity is easily the most underrated feature of a human existence.

OTTO: It is rather small.

ANNA-MARIE: Yes, but it's only a *scale* model.

LARA: I've always dreamed of being known.

LUDWIG: And from next week on you shall be.

OTTO: Isn't it supposed to be something like thirty feet high?

ANNA-MARIE: But it will be!?

LARA: Of being worshipped and adored.

LUDWIG: And little rich girls like you tend to have their dreams come true?

OTTO: And out of bronze?

ANNA-MARIE: And it will be!

LARA: I'm not sure I care for your undergarments.

LUDWIG: Can I not now stop all this ridiculous pointing?

OTTO: And besides it looks nothing at all like him.

ANNA-MARIE: My men start work on the moulding tomorrow.

LARA: How I long to spend time with a man who has actually got to where he's got through hard work and killing people, not because he was, as I was, shunted out of the snatch of some entitled, loveless, blue-blooded bitch.

LUDWIG: That's surely no way to talk about your mother?

OTTO: Tonight, my sweet, I am calling in my debt.

ANNA-MARIE: But your impending nuptials?

OTTO: My fiancée finds me utterly repellent.

ANNA-MARIE: As do I.

OTTO: Keep refusing me and you will never find work anywhere in this Empire again!

CROWD: *(Off.) We want Ludwig, we want Ludwig!*

OTTO: Perhaps it's time for you to greet your adoring public?

LUDWIG: When all I want to do is shower them with my spit.

LUDWIG finally relaxes. Starts putting his clothes on.

LARA: Tell me, Ludwig: what's it like to kill a man?

OTTO: Darling, really!

LUDWIG: If I had a full bladder right now I'd happily go out onto the balcony and…

LARA: What's it like to shove a bayonet through another man's heart?

LUDWIG: The first time you throw up.

LARA: You see, I've read all the manuals published by the military.

OTTO: Well, the nation *is* indeed very grateful.

LUDWIG: Something dies inside you.

LARA: You twist it round before you pull it out, yes?

OTTO: Et cetera, et cetera.

LUDWIG: And you can actually *feel* it dying.

LARA: To pull out all the viscera?

OTTO: Since I *am* a little squeamish.

LUDWIG: Then after that it's just a routine part of the job.

LARA: *(Making the move.)* The action a little like this, I believe?

OTTO: …could we not possibly overlook the details?

LUDWIG: It's just like slaughtering swine.

OTTO: I would prefer not to know.

LUDWIG: It's messy and noisy but no sleep is lost.

LARA: Oh, I would so, so love to kill somebody!

A silence as they all look at her.

Look, I've been rattling the bars of the prison of my life from the moment of my birth. Yes, my destiny's been fixed ever since the day my wet nurse held me in her arms, me all panicky and mewling, and she looked in vain for a set of testicles between my pudgy, bloodied legs and delivered in solemn tones the devastating news, 'I'm sorry to report, your Majesty, this baby is a girl.' I was then betrothed to this prancing little tit here when I was barely out of my swaddling bands. I spent my childhood in numerous different palaces but rarely with my parents and so my whole solitary life has been geared towards this moment: moving to your dreadful country and pretending to the world that I love a man whom I met barely a month ago and for whom, if death were to come knocking now and take him away, I would not shed a single solitary tear…

OTTO: Lara, you jest!?

LARA: On the contrary: nobody in this whole Empire, no conquered man or woman anywhere in our soon-to-be-united territories, would be cheering the news louder than I.

LUDWIG: I am now rather warming to you.

LARA: I believe, once I am married to this moron, I shall be taking you as my lover.

LUDWIG: I should warn you I am not a tender man.

LARA: I do not require tenderness.

OTTO: All I ask is that you are both discrete.

CROWD: *(Off.) We want Ludwig, we want Ludwig!*

OTTO: Oh, it sickens me how much they love this man!

LARA: I doubt the turnout for our wedding will be a cause of similar celebration.

OTTO: My father wants to us to capitalise on the good feeling our victory has generated.

CROWD: *(Off.) We want Ludwig, we want Ludwig!*

LUDWIG: Do I really have to go?

OTTO: We will join you out there momentarily.

LUDWIG: How I loathe and detest the common man.

LUDWIG steps out onto a balcony to a rapturous reception.

OTTO: As I was saying, we need to commission another statue.

ANNA-MARIE: You do?

OTTO: One to commemorate our wedding. The two of us in a loving embrace.

ANNA-MARIE: And am I to be considered for the job?

OTTO: I think we might be able to come to some arrangement.

LARA: So this is whom you've set your sights on, is it?

OTTO: I tend to prefer sexual encounters with the lower orders.

LARA: Oh, it must be so awful for you, my dear.

ANNA-MARIE: In what way?

LARA: Well, I don't know: to actually have to work for a living.

OTTO: *(To ANNA-MARIE.)* So, tonight, my poppet, you have a very big decision to make.

86

Hand in hand LARA and OTTO join LUDWIG to wave to the crowd from the balcony.

Much wild cheering.

ANNA-MARIE: I must now find myself a freezing attic room. And a length of rope. And there I will hang myself from the eaves and remain swinging until the stench of my rotting flesh alerts someone. Or the rats and the maggots have picked my bones clean. I shall die as I have lived: alone. Alone and unknown. But I shall have no regrets. I have always had my art. My art has always, always kept me warm. No, they will never take my art away from me. I will never let them take away my art.

She rips the clay statue to pieces.

VI. PUNCHING DOWN IN PATRIARCHAL SOCIETIES

SIR PHILIP is reading by the fire. LADY MARY (heavily pregnant) is embroidering. They do not speak for a time.

LADY MARY: I was just thinking, darling…

He holds up his hand. A silence as he reads on and she embroiders.

It's so nice to have you back home because…

He holds up his hand. A silence as he reads on and she embroiders.

It's been so lonely here without you and…

He holds up his hand. A silence as he reads on and she embroiders.

What book is it that you are…?

SIR PHILIP: I should very much like, if you will permit me, to reach the end of this current chapter.

LADY MARY: Of course. I beg your pardon.

A silence as he reads on and she embroiders.

I can't remember the last time we two sat together like this by the…

He holds up his hand. A silence as he reads on and she embroiders.

Darling, I have for so long craved your company and your conversation that….

SIR PHILIP: I am on the final paragraph now so…

LADY MARY: I understand.

A silence as he reads on and she embroiders.

I felt our son and heir kicking this morning, darling.
He was kicking with such life and such…

SIR PHILIP: *(Closing the book.)* This is a book on witchcraft.

LADY MARY: Witchcraft?

SIR PHILIP: Penned by none other than his Majesty the King.

LADY MARY: I do so worry about your relationship with that man.

KING JAMES: *(Voiceover, Scots:)* 'The fearful abounding at this
time in this country of these detestable slaves of the Devil
has moved me to resolve the doubting both that such
assaults of Satan are most certainly practised, and that the
instrument thereof merits most severely to be punished.'

LADY MARY: For I have long believed he is rather in love
with you.

SIR PHILIP: He is not at all in love with me!

LADY MARY: He wants to visit us so often and his constant
visits are quickly emptying our coffers.

SIR PHILIP: It is worth the expense for my potential
advancement at the Court.

LADY MARY: But your *potential* advancement at the Court has
not yet translated into *actual* advancement.

SIR PHILIP: But it will, it will…

LADY MARY: And it is quite sinful that a monarch, a man who
is married with children, should so shamelessly flaunt his
preference for all his bright young boys.

SIR PHILIP: He is a man who is simply more comfortable
amongst other men.

LADY MARY: That much is obvious.

SIR PHILIP: He is a man who in truth despises women.

LADY MARY: That the King of England should be a Scottish
sodomite, Philip!

SIR PHILIP: Fear not, I shan't be succumbing to his invitations.

LADY MARY: You succumbing to *his* invitations is not my chief concern.

SIR PHILIP: What do you mean by that?

LADY MARY: You know perfectly well what I mean.

SIR PHILIP: Oh, not this Lucy business again.

LADY MARY: I have seen the way you look at her.

SIR PHILIP: I'm going to retire if you persist with this.

LADY MARY: And I know I am heavy with child now and that she is so young and so pretty...

SIR PHILIP: Once and for all I am interested neither in the body of the King of England nor in that of our simple little serving maid!

LADY MARY: Do you swear?

SIR PHILIP: Of course I do.

LADY MARY: Oh, darling, I'm sorry for doubting all the time but it's been so lonely here these last few months and we hardly ever see you...

SIR PHILIP: Well, you are seeing me *now*.

LADY MARY: I cannot help but believe you are only back here in the country at this time because of the dreadful pestilence ravaging London and not because you wish to spend time with the wife who adores you.

SIR PHILIP: The King believes we are being visited by this latest pestilence because we have failed to deal sufficiently harshly with all these witches in our realm, this army of Satan's helpers who are everywhere and amongst us and who are working tirelessly to destroy the Christian Faith in our lands...

LADY MARY: Well, if it *has* been this current outbreak of
    plague that has brought you home to me then in a way
    I suppose I am grateful for it.

SIR PHILIP: You don't remotely mean that!

LADY MARY: I know, I know, you will now tell me that I have
    everything: I am the mistress of this wonderful house, that
    I have an army of servants about me tending to my every
    whim, that I have everything that money can buy...

SIR PHILIP: I do all I can to make you happy!

LADY MARY: And yet I always feel like a caged bird.

SIR PHILIP: I give you everything you desire, Mary! Everything!

LADY MARY: But even your adored falcons and hawks you
    keep for hunting are occasionally allowed to fly free.
    Not so I. Sometimes it feels that even a girl like Lucy has
    more freedom than I do. She at least has her friends and
    co-workers about her. I feel like I am almost as one of
    your mares, one of your hounds, carefully selected for the
    purposes of breeding. I am here merely to continue your
    famous line and it's as if I am not permitted a personality
    of my own. All I do is read and embroider and stare out
    of the window and I miss you so much and, if you really
    want the truth, I am jealous, Philip. So bitterly jealous.
    I worry that when you're away from me, and with so
    many ambitious young women in London, that you will
    show that weakness once again which so nearly...

SIR PHILIP: I am yours, Mary. I am now and forever all
    yours.

LADY MARY: For I do so love you.

SIR PHILIP: And I love you.

LADY MARY: You swear to me on the life of this unborn child
    you will always be true?

SIR PHILIP: You are the only woman I have ever had any interest in.

LUCY enters.

LUCY: Will there be anything else, my Lord?

LADY MARY: We were both about to retire so…

SIR PHILIP: What about a drop of wine before bed?

LADY MARY: I do not think in my condition that…

SIR PHILIP: Then *you* go up to bed, my darling, and I will join you very shortly.

LADY MARY: You may now retire yourself, Lucy.

SIR PHILIP: After she has poured me my wine she can.

LADY MARY: Well, *I* can pour your wine for you.

LUCY: I am happy to…

LADY MARY: If you would kindly speak when you are spoken to, girl!

SIR PHILIP: No need to be rude to her.

LADY MARY: I wasn't at all being rude to her.

SIR PHILIP: If you would care to fill me up?

LUCY: Of course, my Lord.

LADY MARY: I shall do it, Lucy!

SIR PHILIP: My darling, what is the purpose of having servants if we ourselves perform the tasks they are kept to perform?

LADY MARY: Because I am more than capable of pouring wine for my own husband.

SIR PHILIP: But your own husband is commanding you not to.

LADY MARY: He may well be commanding me not to but I insist that…

SIR PHILIP: *(A sudden rage.)* Your husband is currently commanding you not to!!

A silence.

LADY MARY: And on that note I shall go up to my bed.

SIR PHILIP: Please, my love. I didn't mean to lose my temper.

LADY MARY: I will *not* be shouted at in front of this surly creature here who should, if I had my way, no longer be in our service!

She storms out.

A silence.

LUCY: Shall I pour you the wine, sir?

SIR PHILIP: Yes, please, Lucy. That would be most welcome.

He watches her intently as she pours the wine.

Please don't trouble yourself about Lady Davenport and her dark moods.

LUCY: No, sir.

SIR PHILIP: She grows very weary now that the birth of our son approaches.

LUCY: May I be permitted to say something, sir?

SIR PHILIP: Of course you may.

LUCY: My life here is becoming harder and harder now that your mistress seems to loathe me more with each passing day.

SIR PHILIP: She has a temper, yes, but…

LUCY: She seems to want to work me to death.

SIR PHILIP: In what way?

LUCY: Yesterday, although William and Sam were both doing nothing at all, she made me chop wood out in the yard in the driving rain and then carry it all single-handedly inside.

SIR PHILIP: I shall speak to her.

LUCY: I try so hard to please but nothing I do seems to make her happy.

SIR PHILIP: Perhaps you are trying too hard?

LUCY: Your wine, sir.

He takes it.

Will there be anything else?

SIR PHILIP: This is an Italian vintage.

He drinks deep.

LUCY: Sir?

SIR PHILIP: Yes?

LUCY: Will there be anything else?

SIR PHILIP: Would you like to try some?

LUCY: I'm not really a great drinker of wine so…

SIR PHILIP: Please. Taste it. It will transport you out of this plague-infested country and over to the blue-skies of an enchanting Umbrian hillside.

LUCY: If it pleases you, sir.

She drinks from the cup.

SIR PHILIP: You know you are a very striking-looking girl, Lucy.

LUCY: Thank you, sir.

SIR PHILIP: And tell me: do I please *you* at all?

LUCY: In what way, sir?

SIR PHILIP: You know perfectly well in what way.

LUCY: I don't think I do.

SIR PHILIP: Does the way I look please you? My form? My face? The shape of me, so to speak?

She does not speak.

Why do you not speak, Lucy?

LUCY: I don't know what you want me to say.

SIR PHILIP: I want to hear you say…

LUCY: Say what, my Lord?

SIR PHILIP: Well, that you find me attractive.

LUCY: You are a…

SIR PHILIP: Yes?

LUCY: You are a man, my lord.

SIR PHILIP: I am a man?

LUCY: Indeed.

SIR PHILIP: But what kind of man?

LUCY: Please, my Lord.

SIR PHILIP: Tell me: do you like the wine?

LUCY: I think so, sir.

SIR PHILIP: Your mistress, I believe, is always a little uneasy when you and I are together under the same roof because she believes that…

LUCY: Why should that be, sir?

SIR PHILIP: I was trying to explain.

LUCY: I'm sorry, sir.

SIR PHILIP: She senses that there is…I don't know…a deep attraction between the two of us and so…

LUCY: A deep attraction?

SIR PHILIP: And isn't she right?

LUCY: I don't know what you mean.

SIR PHILIP: Because I am *deeply* attracted to you, Lucy.

LUCY: You are?

SIR PHILIP: And you, I sense, at least in little part return my feelings.

LUCY: Please, sir, don't do this.

SIR PHILIP: Don't do what, Lucy?

LUCY: Don't come any closer.

SIR PHILIP: Why not?

LUCY: You are scaring me.

SIR PHILIP: How?

LUCY: The way you're looking at me.

SIR PHILIP: How am I looking at you?

LUCY: Your eyes are cold, your eyes are cruel.

SIR PHILIP: Do you find me desirable?

LUCY: Desirable?

SIR PHILIP: Yes. Desirable, Lucy.

LUCY: You want the truth?

SIR PHILIP: I always want the truth.

LUCY: Then no, sir. I do not.

A silence.

SIR PHILIP: Not in any way desirable?

LUCY: Not in any way desirable, my Lord.

SIR PHILIP: I now feel most unhappy.

LUCY: I do not mean to make you feel unhappy, sir.

SIR PHILIP: It's like the blood is draining from my body.

LUCY: May I go now?

SIR PHILIP: Because I want you, Lucy, and I mean to have you.

LUCY: I really would like to go now.

SIR PHILIP: And, ever since I was a boy, I have been used
to having what I desire. It is the way I was raised, you
understand? My parents always assured me the world was
my plaything and that I should simply take whatsoever it
was I wanted from it.

LUCY turns to go but SIR PHILIP grabs her by the sleeve.

LUCY: I shall scream, sir.

SIR PHILIP: *(Producing a dagger.)* If you utter a sound I shall
slice your throat with this.

He pushes her down on her back.

LUCY: I beg you, sir!

SIR PHILIP: You belong to me. Remember that, yes? You belong to me, you are my property and therefore I shall do with you whatever I desire.

He rapes her.

LUCY: *(During this.)* Then I saw a new heaven and a new earth for the first heaven and the first earth had passed away, and there was no longer any sea. I saw the Holy City, the new Jerusalem, coming down out of heaven from God, prepared as a bride beautifully dressed for her husband. And I heard a loud voice from the throne saying, 'Look! God's dwelling place is now among the people, and he will dwell with them. They will be his people, and God himself will be with them and be their God. He will wipe every tear from their eyes. There will be no more death or mourning or crying or pain, for the old order of things has passed away.'

SIR PHILIP: There now. This was all your doing. You tempted me on to it with those devilish eyes of yours.

She stands.

You may go. And breathe not a word of this to anyone.

She stares hard at him.

What are you waiting for, girl? I said, you may go!

LUCY: I curse you, Philip Davenport. And no, I shall never again call you 'sir'! I curse you and your wife, and most of all I curse your unborn child. May it fall sick and die in its crib. I curse you and all your wretched line. May everything you touch fall and tumble, may all your ambitions be thwarted. May you die alone and unloved and forgotten and then for an eternity may you reside with Lucifer and his demons and then may you burn, burn, burn in Hell!

She rushes out.

LADY MARY (no longer pregnant) kneeling before a crib.

LADY MARY: My dear little cherub, hold fast to this life. My darling love, just please keep breathing. That's right, that's right. Let me see that smile again. Come on, Charlie, you can do it for Mama. You can open those big blue eyes. Open those eyes for your mother, my love. And let me once again hear that magnificent, life-loving, window-rattling roar.

LUCY enters.

Come here, Lucy. Come look at my boy.

LUCY cautiously approaches.

Is what my husband tells me true?

LUCY: What did he tell you?

LADY MARY: That you laid a curse upon my child?

LUCY: I was very angry.

LADY MARY: So you confess that you committed this wicked deed?

LUCY: I'm sorry…

LADY MARY: Why would you do such a thing?

LUCY: Your husband upset me.

LADY MARY: In what regard?

LUCY: It doesn't matter now.

LADY MARY: How did he upset you so that you thought fit to call down a curse upon our happiness?

LUCY: I'd prefer not to say.

LADY MARY: I demand that you tell me!

LUCY: He said I would lose my position if I speak of it.

LADY MARY: You will lose your position if you do not!

A silence.

LUCY: He…He…

LADY MARY: Yes?

LUCY: He forced himself upon me, madam.

A silence.

LADY MARY: I don't believe you.

LUCY: It's the truth as God is my witness.

LADY MARY: And so this is why you…?

LUCY: I was not in control of my words.

LADY MARY: Lift this curse, Lucy, I beg you!

LUCY: Your baby is not cursed!

LADY MARY: If you lift this curse and he lives…

LUCY: There is a great sickness sweeping the land!

LADY MARY: …we shall pretend that none of this ever happened.

LUCY: But I don't know how to!

LADY MARY: Come to the crib now and do something, anything, to save my darling boy!

LUCY: Lady Davenport, please…

LADY MARY: Approach, approach…

LUCY cautiously approaches the crib.

LUCY: I shall not be able to save him.

LADY MARY: Cast a spell or give a potion or...

LUCY: It is hopeless, Madam.

LADY MARY: Do not say such a thing!

LUCY: Your son is dying and there is nothing at all can be done! Nothing, nothing!

LUCY rushes out as LADY MARY sinks to her knees in prayer.

*

LADY MARY is lifted to her feet by SIR PHILIP.

SIR PHILIP: The trial of Lucy Mayhew is now over, my beloved.

LADY MARY: Yes?

SIR PHILIP: And how honoured we have been to have the King himself presiding over the case for us.

LADY MARY: What was the verdict?

SIR PHILIP: They are even now lighting the bonfire.

LADY MARY: Her death will never bring our Charlie back.

SIR PHILIP: Charlie awaits us both in paradise.

LADY MARY: Then let me go to him now!

SIR PHILIP: We will have other Charlies.

LADY MARY: There will be no other Charlies!

SIR PHILIP: We will have other children. We will have many other children.

A bonfire is lit in the yard.

Do you wish to attend? The King is lighting the faggots out there.

LUCY screams off.

LADY MARY: I do not wish to watch a woman burn to death.

LUCY: *(Off.)* I recant, I recant, I recant!

SIR PHILIP: You are trembling, my love. Let me hold you.

LADY MARY: Do not dare to touch me, you monster!

SIR PHILIP: My darling?

LADY MARY: I do not want you anywhere near me ever again!

LUCY: *(Off.)* Please, please, I still have so much life inside me! So much life to live, so much love, so much love to give!

LUCY screams again and LADY MARY covers her ears.

KING JAMES: *(Voiceover, Scots:)* Go gi' yer love to the Devil, yer dark-hearted sorceress!

LUCY: Your Majesty, please have mercy, please!

KING JAMES: *(Voiceover, Scots:)* There'll be no mercy for ye here! So burn, burn, yer wicked wee lassie! Burn!

LUCY screams terribly.

SIR PHILIP: You see, my darling? The world is shortly to be lighter of a little more evil.

VII.   THE THINGS WE DO FOR LOVE

It is night. HACKER is loading the quartered sections of a Catholic priest, freshly executed, onto a cart.

HACKER: I tell you some'at: as a lad I never fought I'd end
up doin' a job like this. 'Ackin' up priests and that. Luggin'
bits of 'em about afterwards, so's their chops can be taken
to the four quarters of the land and set up on spikes or
dangled over castle walls. Yeah, I actually 'ad dreams
of 'igher matters…Never known exactly what I wannid
'ado o' course but I 'ad much 'igher 'opes for meself than
this. I mean, me old man were a butcher, wannee, wanid
me to take over from 'im, so I got a bit o' experience o'
dealin' out death and hackin' up flesh and I tell yer what,
when you stick a knife frough a pig's froat he makes a lot
more racket than your average traitor does. I mean, your
average traitor, 'e usually just chunters to imself, dunnee,
all the while prayin' and whatnot, fiddlin' with 'is stupid
fuckin' beads an' that or doin' all this bollocks.

He crosses himself.

But a pig or a cow or a chicken, I tell yer, a pig or a cow or
a chicken they don't wanna die. I mean, they *really* don't
wanna die. Not one single part of 'em wants to be roastin'
on a spit or served up with spuds and cabbage. They kick
and they squeal and they shit themselves and their eyes
pop out their 'eads and they do all they can to cling onto
this life but your priest, I tell yer, your priest seems to just
wanna go, seems to welcome the flames or the 'angman's
noose. Or the axe. A pig *loves* life. A priest…well, that's
another fuckin' story, innit.

He holds up a human head.

Take this prelate today. 'e actually fuckin fanks me. Looks
me right in the eye, all serene and smilin' like and, yeah,

'e actually fanks me. I'm putting the noose 'round is neck, the crowd are all goin' nuts and jeerin' and frowin' shit at 'im, you know, any manner o' shit as could be found on the ground and 'e just smiles like I'm doin' 'im the biggest fuckin' favour in the world. It's bizarre, I tell yer. And then a stone gets lobbed over, just fuckin' missin' *me*, which left me right rankled I can tell yer, and its 'im right 'ere, look, right 'ere on is snout 'ere and crack, you can tell it's broken and the blood's comin' out in bright red streams and still 'e's fankin' me and sayin' God be with you, my son, and one day we'll meet again in Christ and whatnot and I tell yer soming: I don't know what these people fink and that, I don't know why they believe so strongly what they believe, I mean, that they believe it so much they actually wanna fuckin' die for it but if I go to my death when my time comes with alf the bollocks as this old boy then I'll be an 'appy man, I guess.

He looks at the head.

I mean, 'e only seemed scared for a bit. You know, at the point when I'm cutting 'im down from the rope and sharpenin' me knives an that. And when I start slicin' out 'is innards and spoolin' it all out of 'im, well, 'is squeals were a bit swine-like then. He's fadin' in and out of it. The life slowly drainin' out of 'im. And, see, 'cos I took a likin' to 'im I sorta 'urried that bit frough. Went straight to the 'ead choppin. Not me best work today, look. Took a bit of sawin' and hackin'. I was keen, you see, to make it quick but because I was so keen I rushed it and I fink I really did 'urt 'im. Made a right mess of his neck and shoulder blades. But yer live and yer learn, don't yer? That's what I always say, yer live and yer learn.

He throws the head up in the air and catches it.

'ead's goin on London Bridge o' course. Left-arm quarter to Carlisle, right-arm quarter to York, left-leg quarter to Oxford and I dunno where the fourth bit's goin. Some shitty seaport on the south coast, as I recall. Southampton or Plymouth or fuck knows where.

Enter MRS FITZWILLIAM, finely dressed.

Who the fuck are you?

FITZWILLIAM: I am Mrs Elizabeth Fitzwilliam.

HACKER: How d'you get in here?

FITZWILLIAM: And kindly watch your tongue.

HACKER: I said, how d'you get in?

FITZWILLIAM: I bribed the oiks outside.

HACKER: What you mean, you bribed them?

FITZWILLIAM: You people are known for your moral bankruptcy, are you not?

HACKER: Whose morals are more bankrupt, the one what accepts the bribe or the one what fuckin' offers it?

FITZWILLIAM: What's that you're holding?

He shows her the head.

She screams.

HACKER: *(Laughing.)* Friend of yours, is 'e?

FITZWILLIAM: *In nomine Patris et Filii et Spiritus Sancti.*

She opens her eyes to find HACKER holding the head very close to her and speaking for it.

HACKER: *(As the head.) Amen,* my child.

FITZWILLIAM: I'm going to be sick.

HACKER: Weren't you present at the butcherin this afternoon?

FITZWILLIAM: I attempted to be here to offer comfort and
support to the dearest friend I have ever known in this
world but alas...

HACKER: It was *you* he was waving at, wannit?

FITZWILLIAM: Today he attained the grace of our Lord Jesus
Christ.

HACKER: Just before I 'oisted 'im up.

She fights her growing nausea.

Yeah, well, 'e certainly went to meet his Maker wiv guts.
Well, not literally o' course 'cos I removed his *actual* guts,
didn' I, and fed 'em to the crows, but metaphorical guts.
Yeah, 'e 'ad an impressive spirit.

FITZWILLIAM: He did.

HACKER: You were the bird what scarpered, right? The one
he was wavin' at and who legged it before the show got
itself properly started.

FITZWILLIAM: I could not endure it.

HACKER: You were only *watchin'*, love! 'e was the one what
was actually sufferin' it.

He throws her the head, which she catches.

She battles her growing nausea.

Barely recognisable, innee?

FITZWILLIAM: I loved him more than any man alive.

HACKER: I fought they wasn't allowed to get busy with the
birds, like?

FITZWILLIAM: Our love for each other was a communion with Christ.

HACKER: Well, I'd keep yer Papist love to yourself, if I was you, 'cos we're doin' a couple more o' yer tomorrer.

FITZWILLIAM: Father Baines and Father Thomas.

HACKER: Rings a bell.

FITZWILLIAM: Two more martyrs in heaven.

HACKER: They're queuin' up, they are.

FITZWILLIAM: These are barbarous times.

HACKER: But I ain't complainin 'cos I get me basic wage, dun' I, plus a little bonus per 'ead, if you don't mind me makin' a little joke, miss.

FITZWILLIAM: Where are his quarters?

HACKER: His quarters?

FITZWILLIAM: I want his bits.

HACKER: 'is bits?

FITZWILLIAM: I want to take his bits away.

HACKER: 'is bits are for the spike and chain.

FITZWILLIAM: And bury his bits on hallowed ground.

HACKER: 'is bits are for public display.

FITZWILLIAM: I have an accomplice outside who is transporting them for me.

HACKER: 'is bits are meant to deter the Papists.

FITZWILLIAM: And we are willing to pay for any extra help so…

HACKER: 'is bits are for the rooks and kites.

FITZWILLIAM: We are wealthy people and are willing to pay.

HACKER: You know 'ow 'ard it is to secure gainful employment these days?

FITZWILLIAM: My people are the ones being persecuted.

HACKER: Don't sound like you ever done an 'ard day's graft in yer life.

FITZWILLIAM: I have inherited money it is true…

HACKER: Course you 'ave, course you 'ave…

FITZWILLIAM: But I try to use this money for the public good.

HACKER: If I let you take 'is bits, miss, and they found out, they'd 'ang me up and let me rot before you could say…

FITZWILLIAM: I will pay enough for you to make safe passage abroad.

HACKER: …five Hail Marys.

FITZWILLIAM: Tonight we sail for Spain.

HACKER: I never been abroad.

FITZWILLIAM: And there you could find another trade.

HACKER: I could grow lemons.

FITZWILLIAM: Almonds?

HACKER: Oranges?

FITZWILLIAM: Dates.

HACKER: I could get meself off of this rain-sodden island.

FITZWILLIAM: So will you help?

HACKER: What you offer me mates out there?

FITZWILLIAM: The same.

HACKER: Little fuckers.

FITZWILLIAM: They are waiting with my accomplice beyond these walls.

HACKER: Well, a life far from these pestilential shores does 'ave appeal.

FITZWILLIAM: I'm offering you blue skies, red wine, cicadas chirping from the olive trees.

HACKER: But the problem I have with foreign countries boils down to this.

FITZWILLIAM: What?

HACKER: They're fulla fuckin foreigners.

FITZWILLIAM: We don't have much time.

HACKER: So I might want some'ing else from you.

FITZWILLIAM: Something else?

HACKER: To clinch the deal.

FITZWILLIAM: I'm offering you a new life in the sun.

HACKER: I know you are.

FITZWILLIAM: Tell me what you want then.

HACKER: I want *you*.

FITZWILLIAM: Me?

HACKER: I want you to take my fing in yer gob.

FITZWILLIAM: We don't have time for this.

HACKER: And then I fink I'd probably follow yer to the ends of the earth.

FITZWILLIAM: I would never lower myself to even…

He unsheathes his sword.

HACKER: Otherwise I'll stick this in you here and now.

FITZWILLIAM: How dare you threaten me!

HACKER: Oh, I dare, I dare…

FITZWILLIAM: I am a high-born woman whereas you…

HACKER: I got two feet of steel 'ere and all you got is yer beautiful eyes.

FITZWILLIAM: …you are nothing but an open sewer of a man!

HACKER: So, what's it to be?

FITZWILLIAM: Please…

HACKER: A coupla minutes to bring me off.

FITZWILLIAM: Don't make me do this…

HACKER: Or an eternity in Hell with yer bloody, bleeding disconnected priest?

A long silence as she thinks.

FITZWILLIAM: May God forgive me.

She places the head on the floor. She kneels down to him, his sword at her head.

HACKER: Today's been my lucky day after all.

As he closes his eyes she takes a dagger from her cloak.

(Laughing.) You're all proper ladies on the outside, in't yer, but when push comes to shove…

With one swift action of her blade she unmans him.

He drops his sword and screams like a stuck pig.

FITZWILLIAM: You're making far too much noise, sir.

HACKER: Jesus Christ, Jesus Christ, Jesus Christ!

FITZWILLIAM: I would of course urge you to confess your sins but since you are nothing but a filthy pagan…

HACKER: What you do? What the fuck you do?

FITZWILLIAM: …you'd only be wasting your breath.

She cuts his throat and he drops twitching to the ground.

Fly to your own damnation, you heretic hound!

HACKER croaks and gurgles.

This a far more pleasing sound than your endless cursing.

HACKER: *(Weakly.)* Help me…

FITZWILLIAM: You are beyond all help.

HACKER: Please help me…

FITZWILLIAM: You choose to die here like a stuck pig rather than broaden your horizons in some foreign land.

HACKER: Please…

FITZWILLIAM: You are, quite frankly, everything that's wrong with this country.

HACKER lies still as FITZWILLIAM picks up the severed head of the priest.

Oh, Father, forgive me my little transgressions here tonight. I kill only to preserve the true religion. Only to honour you in death as in life. You always had such beautiful, beautiful lips.

She kisses the priest's lips just as JOHNS enters.

JOHNS: What in God's name are you doing?

FITZWILLIAM: Nothing.

JOHNS: Were you kissing that head?

FITZWILLIAM: Of course I wasn't!

JOHNS: It looked to me like you were kissing that head.

FITZWILLIAM: I don't care what it looked like.

JOHNS: I thought you belonged to me…?

FITZWILLIAM: I could never love you as much as I love this man.

JOHNS: And why are there men at the gate with their throats cut?

FITZWILLIAM: They would not be bribed.

JOHNS: And who is this lying on the ground?

FITZWILLIAM: So many questions.

JOHNS: You have murdered *three* men!

FITZWILLIAM: They were not men, they were heretics!

JOHNS: And is that the head of the martyred priest?

FITZWILLIAM: It is.

JOHNS: Then we need to go!

FITZWILLIAM: Yes.

JOHNS: The tide leaves in twenty minutes.

FITZWILLIAM: I could get no one to help me.

JOHNS: We will need to dispose of these bodies.

They pick up the corpse of HACKER and load it onto the cart.

I do not like taking my life in my hands like this.

FITZWILLIAM: This earthly life is meaningless.

JOHNS: So you say.

FITZWILLIAM: It is the life to come which signifies.

JOHNS: Even so.

FITZWILLIAM: They would expose the naked corpse of
    this holy man for all their heathen eyes to gawp at. See
    the flesh blacken and decay, see it become food for the
    carrion birds, see it slide from the bone and drop as
    putrid, maggot-riddled slush onto the ground.

JOHNS: So these are the bits of Father Baines?

FITZWILLIAM: This man's as close as we shall ever come to
    the embodiment of Christ!

JOHNS: The bits of the famous Father Thomas Baines?

FITZWILLIAM: Father Baines dies tomorrow.

JOHNS: So who then is this?

FITZWILLIAM: This is Father Hodson.

JOHNS: Father Hodson?

FITZWILLIAM: And, although Father Baines is saintly and
    good, it's Father Hodson here who had within him the real
    spark of the divine…

JOHNS: Father *Francis* Hodson?

FITZWILLIAM: You knew him?

JOHNS: Let me see.

113

FITZWILLIAM: *(Passing him the head.)* You are holding in your hands a most holy thing. *(A pause.)* What on earth is the matter?

JOHNS: I am shaking now, I'm shaking…

FITZWILLIAM: The brain within this head contained all the goodness and the courage of his almost fifty years.

JOHNS: It's him, I know.

FITZWILLIAM: We know it's him.

JOHNS: This man is no martyr, this man is no saint.

FITZWILLIAM: You didn't know him as I did.

JOHNS: This man was a brute.

FITZWILLIAM: He was kindness itself.

JOHNS: And no man of God.

FITZWILLIAM: It is precisely what he was!

JOHNS: This man defiled me!

FITZWILLIAM: You slander him!

JOHNS: The things he'd do to us, the things he would do…

FITZWILLIAM: You are mistaken.

JOHNS: His wicked lust on children, it would never be appeased.

FITZWILLIAM: When my husband died, without this man's guidance, I would have fallen apart.

JOHNS: This demi-devil all my life has haunted my dreams…

FITZWILLIAM: Without this man's devotion…

JOHNS: He preyed on the choirboys, he preyed on the little girls who swept the church floors, who came to him looking for work, he'd force on us such dreadful unnatural acts, even in full view of the Christ on the cross, that afterwards we were no longer children. He would force us, Mrs Fitzwilliam, children as young as five and six, there on the altar to…One day I watched him baptise a baby in the self-same font against which, the day before, he'd brutalised me. Oh, you have no idea, no idea of my suffering at the hands of this man.

FITZWILLIAM: We all of us have our crosses to bear.

JOHNS: He will *not* be buried on hallowed ground.

JOHNS spits into the face of the severed head.

FITZWILLIAM: You will burn in Hell for that.

JOHNS: I've been burning in Hell for fifteen years because of this beast!

JOHNS throws the head down and rushes off.

FITZWILLIAM: *(Retrieving the head.)* And so, my precious love, it is once again you and I. You and I alone in the world. You and I, it is you and I, it is you and I…

She puts the head on the cart and pushes it away.

VIII.   BLOODY WOMEN

A private chamber. KATHERINE pacing, anxiously.

KATHERINE: Oh, I am in such a turmoil. He will be here any minute and as soon as I see him I doubt I shall be able to control myself. There is such passion in me, such desire.

THOMAS enters.

Oh Lord Jesus, help me. The thing I desire more than anything else in this life is to be free from desire.

THOMAS: Is the desire to be free from desire not also a desire?

KATHERINE: Kiss me, Thomas!

THOMAS: Katherine Howard, I want to do such things to you.

KATHERINE: And I want the same.

THOMAS: But if I so much as touch you, it could cost me my life.

KATHERINE: And, more importantly, it could cost me mine.

THOMAS: I think about you all the time.

KATHERINE: And I think about *you.*

THOMAS: So what do we do?

KATHERINE: I really don't know.

THOMAS: I want to marry you, I want to be with you...

KATHERINE: In another life perhaps...

THOMAS: There *is* no other life!

KATHERINE: Oh, God, Thomas, I so, so want you...

THOMAS: Death is a price I think I would be...

KATHERINE: I am so in love with you...

THOMAS: …willing to pay!

KATHERINE: …but to even say these words is likely death.

THOMAS: Let us kiss.

KATHERINE: This is lunacy you being here. We have to stop this. Kiss me!

THOMAS: Yes.

He goes to her. They almost kiss.

KATHERINE: But the old woman is outside! She will be listening through the door.

THOMAS: Then let us be silent.

KATHERINE: You must go!

THOMAS: I have only just arrived.

KATHERINE: Hold me, Thomas!

THOMAS: Come here then…

KATHERINE: *(Breaking away.)* I am not so sure what you feel for me is love.

THOMAS: Stop this torture, Katherine!

KATHERINE: I suspect it is the other thing men always want.

THOMAS: Oh, I don't know if it's love or if it's the other thing…

KATHERINE: Thomas, please…

THOMAS: But all I know is I think about nothing but you all day and all night.

KATHERINE: You remember what they did to Ann, my cousin?

THOMAS: Of course.

KATHERINE: They chopped off her head.

THOMAS: She was a whore!

KATHERINE: She was innocent!

THOMAS: I want you naked on a bed.

KATHERINE: And you are here now trying to make a whore out of me.

THOMAS: Then why invite me to your rooms?

KATHERINE: Because I want what you want.

THOMAS: You confuse me so.

KATHERINE: At court I must play the game.

THOMAS: The way you look at me sometimes.

KATHERINE: And I am lonely in my situation.

THOMAS: The way, when we are with others, you hold my gaze then look away.

KATHERINE: You are an attractive man so…

THOMAS: The way you let your fingers brush against mine…

KATHERINE: But you are my oldest friend.

THOMAS: I should have married you before that stinking old King ever set his sights on you.

KATHERINE: He is not especially stinking.

THOMAS: Not especially?

KATHERINE: No more stinking than most men.

THOMAS: What a fool I was to let you go.

KATHERINE: He is always extremely tender and kind with me.

THOMAS: Stop, please!

KATHERINE: Whatever is the matter?

THOMAS: The thought of that ginger, bearded tub of lard, that tub of lard with the suppurating sores all over his body…

KATHERINE: You do him a disservice, Tom.

THOMAS: The thought of you and him…

KATHERINE: He treats me like I'm his own special angel.

THOMAS: This is all *your* doing.

KATHERINE: In what way?

THOMAS: Were it not for your vaulting ambition and your desperation to be seen at the Court then…

KATHERINE: You too always longed for the Court…

THOMAS: Then you would be my wife and we could now be consummating our…

KATHERINE: Can a man and a woman not ever simply be friends?

THOMAS: Not when they desire each other as much as we two do.

KATHERINE: Is that not a little sad?

THOMAS: It must be then that you are evil.

KATHERINE: Evil? I?

THOMAS: Yes, evil.

KATHERINE: I am not at all evil.

THOMAS: You are toying with me.

KATHERINE: Thomas, I love you like a brother…

THOMAS: Like a brother, please!

KATHERINE: But it's true!

THOMAS: We should run away together.

KATHERINE: They will track us down and hack us to pieces.

THOMAS: I am in a ferment of desire.

KATHERINE: I have had men desiring me all my life. When I was a child my music master…

THOMAS: I will no longer hear of that man…

KATHERINE: He forced himself upon me…

THOMAS: I know, I know…

THOMAS: Kiss me, Katherine!

KATHERINE: No! Yes! I want to, I want, I want to…

THOMAS: Give me those kissable, kissable lips…

KATHERINE: I will not kiss you until…

THOMAS: Not kiss me until?

KATHERINE: We must be patient, my love.

THOMAS: Must we wait for the King to die before we can…?

KATHERINE: What else can we do?

THOMAS: You know it is treason to imagine the death of a king?

KATHERINE: I am not imagining his death, I am simply saying that…

THOMAS: Oh, who knows how long that fat old bastard might live!

KATHERINE: But, Thomas, I know he is growing angry with me.

THOMAS: He is?

KATHERINE: Because I cannot give him a son.

THOMAS: Then you must give him one.

KATHERINE: He comes to me less often now.

THOMAS: I am glad on it.

KATHERINE: He says he is humiliated. He knows that a woman will only conceive a child when she enjoys the sexual act.

THOMAS: And do you?

KATHERINE: And so, because of my barrenness, all the world now takes him for a terrible lover.

THOMAS: And is he?

KATHERINE: That I cannot say.

THOMAS: *(Grabbing her had.) Is* he a terrible lover, Katherine?

KATHERINE: You are hurting me.

THOMAS: For *I* am not a terrible lover.

KATHERINE: I'm sure not.

THOMAS: I have left a trail of satisfied women in my wake throughout my days.

KATHERINE: Let go of me, please!

THOMAS: I need to know what the King is like between the sheets!

KATHERINE: If you would kindly let go of me, Thomas!

He releases her.

THOMAS: I apologise.

KATHERINE: Why do men always treat me so roughly?

THOMAS: Perhaps because you bewitch us so.

KATHERINE: The King is gentle.

THOMAS: Gentle?

KATHERINE: But he lacks...how shall I put it...all firmness.

THOMAS: You mean to say he...?

KATHERINE: He can no longer satisfy a woman in that regard.

THOMAS: This news delights me!

KATHERINE: But what of me and my needs?

THOMAS: Here I am offering to fulfil those needs.

KATHERINE: But if we ever did the act, and I shall admit again it is what I do desire, then we are both as good as lost.

THOMAS: Let's do it now.

KATHERINE: Don't be so reckless, please.

THOMAS: Let us undress and copulate on the floor right this moment! And then let us die in our pleasure, let us die, let us die, let us die!

KATHERINE: You'd better go.

THOMAS: Go?

KATHERINE: Yes! I mean it! This is madness, madness! Lady Rochford! Master Culpepper is ready to depart.

THOMAS: I am not at all ready to depart!

KATHERINE: But depart you must!

THOMAS: With not even a token of your love?

KATHERINE: Here. I have this for you.

She produces a velvet cap. Gives it to him.

But never let it be said I gave it you.

THOMAS: Why not?

KATHERINE: People will misconstrue.

THOMAS: What will they misconstrue?

KATHERINE: They will think that it a love gift. That I…love you.

THOMAS: But you do!

KATHERINE: Oh, yes, yes, yes I do!

THOMAS: Then kiss me.

She battles with herself. They almost kiss. Then she pushes the man out.

KATHERINE: God in Heaven, tell me. Why did you give us these desires but also tell us from our births that such desires are evil? What kind of torturing monster are you?

*

A room in the Tower. KATHERINE is sobbing desperately as SIR ROBERT stands over her. Outside we hear the murmur of a waiting crowd.

SIR ROBERT: I do understand your distress, your Majesty. But I hope you realise that these allegations must be investigated. The King insists upon it. And it falls to me, a man who's all his life sworn to serve both his sovereign and his country to the upmost, it falls to me to lead the investigation.

She continues to sob.

But I do insist that you try to calm down.

She continues to sob.

For it is hard for me to glean the truth when you allow your emotions to get the better of you in this way.

KATHERINE: *(Incoherent.)* I am innocent.

SIR ROBERT: I do apologise, your Majesty, but I did not quite...

KATHERINE: I am innocent, I said!

SIR ROBERT: None of us are wholly innocent, I fear.

KATHERINE: But I did not commit the crime of which I am being accused!

SIR ROBERT: Since we are all fallen souls in the eyes of God.

KATHERINE: What I mean is, I am innocent in *this* case.

SIR ROBERT: Do you agree we are all fallen souls in the eyes of God?

KATHERINE: Naturally but...

SIR ROBERT: And we are all of us prone to certain weaknesses?

KATHERINE: We are merely human so...

SIR ROBERT: And this Thomas Culpepper is a man known to have a certain effect upon the ladies?

KATHERINE: That may be so but I did not succumb to his charms.

SIR ROBERT: So you confess that he *does* have charms?

KATHERINE: We all have charms, do we not?

SIR ROBERT: I am certain *I* do not.

KATHERINE: Really?

SIR ROBERT: I do *not* have charms.

KATHERINE: I'm sure underneath all the…

SIR ROBERT: I have no charm.

KATHERINE: I am supposing that your wife might…?

SIR ROBERT: I have no wife.

KATHERINE: You seem to me to be a man with…

SIR ROBERT: I have neither wife nor charm. I am wholly without charm. I am sans charm. I am, it has been noted on more than one occasion in the past, a thoroughly charmless man.

KATHERINE: But surely there have been some who've found you…?

SIR ROBERT: I do not even possess any *hidden* charm.

KATHERINE: …even once or twice a little bit…

SIR ROBERT: Look all you like: you will find no charm here.

KATHERINE: …charming?

SIR ROBERT: I am void of charm, my coffers of charm lie empty and bare.

KATHERINE: I see.

SIR ROBERT: I neither like nor trust charming people.

KATHERINE: I see how wise that is.

SIR ROBERT: And this Master Culpepper is a man of boundless charm, yes?

KATHERINE: He is an old friend.

SIR ROBERT: Who confesses he *has* visited your private chambers.

KATHERINE: I have known him since I was a girl.

SIR ROBERT: Who confesses he's received the gift of a velvet cap from you.

KATHERINE: It was a gift from one friend to another.

SIR ROBERT: And you warned him he should tell no one that you gifted it?

KATHERINE: I didn't want people to misconstrue.

SIR ROBERT: Misconstrue what, your Majesty?

KATHERINE: To misconstrue things that were not at all the case.

SIR ROBERT: What things might these be?

KATHERINE: That there was anything more than friendship between us.

SIR ROBERT: He also confessed that you and he imagined the death of His Majesty the King.

KATHERINE: That is not so.

SIR ROBERT: And also that you said, were King Henry not alive, that you two might then joyfully consummate your illicit romance?

KATHERINE: There *is* no romance!

SIR ROBERT: But were you free would not Master Culpepper be a man you might marry?

KATHERINE: Were I free then, yes, that might be possible but I am not so…

SIR ROBERT: Once again, girl, you imagine the death of the King!

KATHERINE: I did not!

SIR ROBERT: I greatly fear that you did.

A man screams in terrible agony outside and a crowd cheer.

They are at present eviscerating Master Dereham.

KATHERINE: Dear God in Heaven.

SIR ROBERT: Your husband, was he not?

KATHERINE: He said so, I did not.

SIR ROBERT: There was a pre-contract, though?

KATHERINE: I was a child, he desired me, he put me under certain…

SIR ROBERT: Certain?

KATHERINE: …pressures.

SIR ROBERT: You were not a maid though when you married the King?

KATHERINE: In my *mind* I was still a maid.

SIR ROBERT: But not in your body?

KATHERINE: Can it be a sin when there is no agency?

SIR ROBERT: But you *had* lain with other men?

KATHERINE: They both touched me against my will, they pestered me, I was always without power. I was nothing but an ignorant child, unaware of the wicked ways of the world.

SIR ROBERT: And yet you and your family concealed this fact from the King?

KATHERINE: I was raised always to do as I was told. To be at all times obedient.

SIR ROBERT: And quite right too.

127

KATHERINE: If only we had the strength when we are young to disobey our parents.

SIR ROBERT: Without blind obedience in our children then anarchy would ensue.

KATHERINE: Oh God, what will become of me?

More terrible screams from the man outside.

SIR ROBERT: You loved this man?

KATHERINE: I don't think so.

SIR ROBERT: There are tears in your eyes as you listen to him die?

KATHERINE: He is...

SIR ROBERT: Was.

KATHERINE: ...a friend.

VOICE: *(Off.)* Behold the head of a traitor.

Cheers from outside.

SIR ROBERT: If only you had given the King the son he craves.

KATHERINE: Would that have changed things?

SIR ROBERT: He may well have turned a blind eye to your indiscretions if you were performing your primary function as his Queen.

KATHERINE: My primary function?

SIR ROBERT: That of a brood mare.

KATHERINE: But surely all I could do in that regard was surrender to the will of God?

SIR ROBERT: It is also the will of God that your treachery was discovered.

KATHERINE: My treachery?

SIR ROBERT: Your days are done, Katherine Howard.

KATHERINE: Am I not still 'Your Majesty' to you ?

SIR ROBERT: You must now make peace with Him who created you.

KATHERINE: Perhaps the King will forgive me! I am young and I could give him a son! I could still give him many, many sons!

SIR ROBERT: Oh, my dear, if only you had.

KATHERINE: Then perhaps he would love me again?

SIR ROBERT: Prince Edward is a most sickly boy. Who knows if he will even outlive his father.

THOMAS: *(Off.)* Katherine! Katherine, I love you, Katherine!

SIR ROBERT: And now is it the turn of Master Culpepper.

THOMAS: *(Off.)* They mean to murder me, Katherine!

KATHERINE: Oh, Tom!

SIR ROBERT: You react in the way any woman who loved would react.

KATHERINE: We are innocent.

SIR ROBERT: That word again?

THOMAS: *(Off.)* Be strong, Katherine! Be strong.

KATHERINE: You poor, dear man.

THOMAS: *(Off.)* And we shall meet again in a better world than this!

KATHERINE: I cannot bear it!

THOMAS: *(Off.)* If only we'd actually fucked, Katherine!

KATHERINE: No, no!

THOMAS: *(Off.)* Darling, we are dying and we never even got to fuck!

The sound of an axe falling. Cheering.

VOICE: *(Off.)* Behold the head of another traitor!

SIR ROBERT: And so it would appear that Master Culpepper will have no more need of this.

He produces the velvet cap.

Since I believe it's only those who possess the full complement of heads who require such dainty little velvet caps?

KATHERINE: He didn't deserve this.

SIR ROBERT: You recognise the cap?

KATHERINE: I do.

SIR ROBERT: A token of your love for him, yes?

KATHERINE: I did love him, yes.

SIR ROBERT: At last.

KATHERINE: But love is not a crime, is it? We shouldn't have to die for it!

SIR ROBERT: We are *all* going to die, Katherine.

KATHERINE: I know this but…

SIR ROBERT: You and your lovers have at least been spared the horrors of growing old, of slowly falling apart.

KATHERINE: So I am really to die?

SIR ROBERT: It cannot be avoided.

KATHERINE: When?

SIR ROBERT: At sunrise.

KATHERINE: Then perhaps you will grant me one request?

SIR ROBERT: I shall try.

KATHERINE: Might I spend my final night on this earth
   rehearsing my death?

SIR ROBERT: And how might I assist you in this endeavour?

KATHERINE: Bring me a block. That I might practice how to
   place myself upon it. I should hate to appear afraid before
   all the crowds that will be sure to gather.

SIR ROBERT: They are queuing up already.

KATHERINE: So all I am then is entertainment?

SIR ROBERT: That, my dear lady, has certainly been an
   important part of your role.

KATHERINE: Entertainment?

SIR ROBERT: In this: your pathetically short sojourn upon this
   earth.

*

*KATHERINE alone, circling the block. Outside the sound of a scaffold
being erected, hammering, the odd builder's laugh, the odd builder's
shout.*

KATHERINE: Such a small, innocuous thing. And you are
   to be my solitary companion tomorrow? From which
   wood are you made? I was never any good at naming
   the different trees. Are you oak perhaps? Or pine? I
   believe you must be oak. From a mighty tree growing in

a beautiful, untamed forest. And then they came with their axes and their saws and they chopped you down. For wood to make their ships that sail across the seas and steal from and subdue all the many peoples of this earth. Wood to make their ships, wood to fashion their blocks and wood to build their scaffolds, their scaffolds that help them cut the heads off Queens. But, yes, I sense some life in you still. The same force that fires the blood in me, fires yet a little life in you. And so I feel therefore a little less alone. A little less afraid. I shall lay my head upon you and shall not show any fear. They say they will provide me with a blindfold. So I will not sense exactly when the axe will fall. But also because, once my head is severed from my neck, I will not see the ground rise up. One's vision is maintained, it seems, for several seconds after the blow is struck. So there is yet a little kindness in the King. Kindness in the face of this cold-blooded and calculated act of murder. So let me practice. Let me kneel. No, I must not kneel. I must lie like this. This is not so terrible. And when I am ready do I hold out my arms like so? So that the man in the mask will know when to strike. And then I say my prayers and…Oh God, no, no! *(Rising.)* I really don't want to die! Please! I am not ready at all to die! I am but a girl! Gaoler! I'm scared! So alone, so endlessly alone in my life! And I don't even think I am pretty. If only

I wasn't considered so pretty. I am an intelligent young woman with my whole life before me! There is surely more to me, so much more to me than just the way I look. But the world of men will never know it. The world of men will never see it. God, are you with me? Are you here with me in this hour? Hold my hand, Lord. Please be merciful and hold my shaking hand.

A light change.

Ah, it is growing light. The stars still visible, look, but the new day is dawning. So it must be time for me to die.

I am now going back home. Back to that great nothingness which has always been. And always *will* be. We are but tiny waves upon a vast ocean. And the waves don't die, do they, as they break upon the shore? They simply become a part of the sea once more. Katherine, Queen of England, will soon be no more, but *I* shall live on. Kath-er-ine. These are merely sounds made by these unhappy lips. Lips that soon shall be stilled and cold forever. Merely three silly syllables. That is not who we are. We are surely more than just our names. More than just our sad little stories on this earth. So let me once again.

She lies down to the block. Stretches out her arms as before.

I am calm, I am calm. All I am is breathing. All I am is gentle breath. I breathe in, I breathe out, I breathe in, I breathe out. And this is all there is. This is all I need. The breath of this one eternal moment. And in and out and in and out. Now you see me, now you don't, now you see me, now you don't, now you see me…

The sound of an axe falling in the darkness.